MADHUR JAFFREY'S
QUICK & EASY
INDIAN
COOKING

PHOTOGRAPHY BY
PHILIP SALAVERRY

For Rohan Kaelin Jaffrey

■ ■ ■ ■ ■ ■ ■

I would like to thank a small group of dear friends,
Badi, Chun, and Draupadiji, as well as my sister Lalit
who helped me with these recipes.

MADHUR JAFFREY'S

QUICK & EASY

INDIAN

COOKING

PHOTOGRAPHY BY

PHILIP SALAVERRY

CHRONICLE BOOKS

SAN FRANCISCO

Book Design: Mitten Design
Food Stylist: Sue White
Prop Stylist: Amy Glenn
Photographer's Assistant: Shane Neil
Food Stylist's Assistants: Dan Becker and Andrea Lucich
Prop Stylist's Assistant: Anthony Juerte

The photographer wishes to thank: Aude Bronson-Howard, NYC; Cyclamen Studios Berkeley, Julie Sanders
Designer; Ward Finer; Bea and Marty Glenn; Nancy Glenn; Rosie and Harry Glenn-Finer; Anabel Glenn-
Schuster; J. Goldsmith Antiques Prop Shop; Mini Koch Backgrounds; Merna Oeberst; Daniel Schuster; Sue
Fisher King; V. Breier Gallery; Judy and Bernie Carrasco. (All locations are San Francisco unless specified.)

Library of Congress Cataloging-in-Publication Data:

Jaffrey, Madhur.
    Madhur Jaffrey's quick and easy Indian cooking / photography by Philip Salaverry.
        p. cm.
    Includes index.
    ISBN 0-8118-1183-2
    1. Cookery, India. 2. Quick and easy cookery. I. Title.
TX724.5.I4J29 1996
641.5954--dc20   95-31296
             CIP

Printed in Hong Kong.

Distributed in Canada by Raincoast Books, 8680 Cambie St., Vancouver, B.C. V6P 6M9

10 9 8 7 6 5 4 3 2 1

Chronicle Books, 275 Fifth Street, San Francisco, CA 94103

CONTENTS

■■■■■■■

■■■■■■■

INTRODUCTION

■■■■■■

"Are there any Indian recipes that are quick and easy?" I am asked this question often. You have only to come to my home for dinner to know that there are hundreds of them. You have to come during a weekday when I am also writing for twelve to fourteen hours (or acting or gardening) and have barely time to sneeze. My husband and I eat well, even on those days.

Let's face it: There is no way to get instant marvelous food. If that is what you want, it can only be had at a restaurant (and not always there) or in somebody else's home. But this book may help you come close. Some effort has to be expended in having a well-stocked pantry and in some daily shopping. After that, there will be some chopping and stirring, but this can all be done, on the whole, within thirty minutes.

The secret lies in not being too ambitious. Have just a satisfying soup and salad for lunch and perhaps a *vindaloo,* plain rice, and quickly stir-fried vegetables for dinner. For breakfast on Sundays there are wonderfully spicy omelets to be had, and for tea, how about onion fritters?

Do not be afraid to combine Indian main courses with Western side dishes: spicy fried fish with boiled potatoes and a green salad, an egg curry with toast. Indian breads are somewhat complicated to make, so get them from your local Indian restaurant to go with your homemade kebab or curry.

Also, do not be afraid of the long list of spices in some recipes. I have stayed away from dishes that require a lot of stirring or have too many steps. But stay away from too many spices? That would be like asking an Indian not to be an Indian! If you can put one spice into a pan, you can just as easily put in ten or even fifteen. They will all cook quickly and easily. I can assure you of that.

NOTES ON THE RECIPES
∎∎∎∎∎∎∎

With a few exceptions, the recipes in this book can be prepared and cooked within thirty minutes. Occasionally this calls for a pressure cooker, but its use is not essential. The cooking time will be longer without one, but the ingredients are quickly and easily prepared and the actual cooking methods are simple.

Spices and seasonings are available from Indian stores and many supermarkets. Ingredients are also available through mail-order sources, including the following:

Bombay Emporium
294 Craft Avenue
Pittsburgh, PA 15213
412.682.4965

India Spices and Grocery
5891 W. Pico Boulevard
Los Angeles, CA 90010
213.931.4871

Food of India Sinha Trading Company
121 Lexington Avenue
New York, NY 10016
212.683.4419

The Souk
1916 Pike Place N
Seattle, WA 98101
206.441.1666

India Gifts and Food
1031 W. Belmount Avenue
Chicago, IL 60657
312.348.4393

SOUPS, APPETIZERS, AND SNACKS

∎∎∎∎∎∎∎

The premise of this book does not suggest that you sit down to three-course meals, but my own feeling is, why not have the choice? The soups may be had by themselves for lunch, the chicken and shrimp dishes may be served with drinks, and the onion fritters and sandwiches may be eaten with tea. But if you feel like putting together several quick-cooking dishes to make up a grander dinner, these recipes will help you out with the first course.

∎∎∎∎∎∎∎

·······

·······

GINGERY CAULIFLOWER SOUP

Gobi ka soup

■ ■ ■ ■ ■ ■

This soup may be served as an elegant first course at a grand dinner or as part of a simple lunch accompanied, perhaps, by a sandwich or salad or both. It may be made a day in advance and refrigerated. Reheat gently.

It is a good idea to have the cumin, coriander, turmeric, and cayenne pepper all measured into a small bowl before you start, as they go in together and cook very briefly.

INGREDIENTS

3 tablespoons vegetable oil

1 medium size onion (about 6 ounces) peeled and chopped

1-inch piece fresh ginger, peeled and cut into fine slivers

4 cloves garlic, peeled and chopped

1 teaspoon ground cumin

2 teaspoons ground coriander

¼ teaspoon ground turmeric

⅛ to ¼ teaspoon cayenne pepper

2 medium potatoes, peeled and cut into rough ⅓-inch dice

½ pound (2 heaping cups) cauliflower florets

5 cups chicken stock

Salt if needed

⅔ cup heavy, whipping cream

Set the oil over medium-high heat in a good-sized saucepan. When hot, put in the onion, ginger, and garlic. Stir and fry for about 4 minutes or until the onion is somewhat browned. Put in the cumin, coriander, turmeric, and cayenne pepper. Stir once and put in the potatoes, cauliflower, and chicken stock. If the stock is unsalted, put in ¾ teaspoon salt. Stir and bring to a boil. Cover, turn the heat to low, and simmer gently for 10 minutes or until the potatoes are tender. Taste for salt, adding more if you like.

Put the soup into a blender, in 2 batches or more as required, and blend thoroughly. Strain, pushing down to get all the pulp. Add the cream and mix. The soup may now be reheated and served.

SERVES 4–6

A LIGHT, COLD YOGURT SOUP

Safed shorva

■■■■■■

A light, delightful cold soup for a warm summer day. And, it needs no cooking! I tend to make mine with low-fat yogurt but you could just as easily use the creamier variety.

If you are in a hurry, you could chop up the tomato without peeling it, but it is preferable—and it does not take that much longer—to peel and seed it first. To do this, just toss a large tomato into boiling water for 15 seconds and then remove the skin. Cut the tomato in half, crosswise, and gently squeeze out all the seeds. Now dice the shell.

If you are using homemade chicken stock for this recipe, make sure that it comes straight out of the refrigerator. Strain it so that no particles of congealed fat fall into the soup.

Ingredients

2½ cups plain yogurt	2 teaspoons finely chopped fresh mint or cilantro
4 cups chicken stock	(Chinese parsley, fresh green coriander) or a mixture of both
½ teaspoon peeled and very finely grated fresh ginger	Salt to taste
½ cup peeled and finely diced cucumber	Freshly ground black pepper
½ cup peeled, seeded, and finely diced tomato	
⅛ teaspoon cayenne pepper	

Put the yogurt in a bowl. Beat with a fork until smooth and creamy. Slowly add the stock, mixing it as you do so. Add all the remaining ingredients and mix. Refrigerate until needed. Stir well before serving.

SERVES 4

DELICIOUS CHICKEN BITS
Murgh ke mazedar tukray

■ ■ ■ ■ ■ ■

These wonderful chicken cubes may be served hot, warm, or cold. They may be pierced with toothpicks and nibbled with drinks, added to salads, or eaten at picnics. The last is what I did most recently just before I watched my youngest daughter perform the part of Miranda in a summer production of Shakespeare's *Tempest,* set in a park. (The chicken bits may also be eaten as a main course with rice or potatoes and a green salad; the recipe will then serve four.)

You may be surprised by my use of thyme. It tastes somewhat like our *ajwain* seeds, which are much harder to find. If you can get these, use about ⅓ teaspoon only as they are quite strong in flavor. The spice mixture I have used here is an excellent one to have on hand. It may be mixed in advance in the correct proportions (just the dry seasonings, not the oil) and then used when grilling fish, steaks, and chops.

INGREDIENTS

1¼ pounds boned, skinned chicken breasts (4 breast pieces)
1 teaspoon freshly ground black pepper
¼ teaspoon ground turmeric
¼ teaspoon cayenne pepper
1 teaspoon ground cumin
1 teaspoon dried thyme or ½ teaspoon ajwain seeds (see recipe introduction)

¼ teaspoon garlic powder
1 teaspoon bright red paprika
¾ teaspoon salt
About 3 tablespoons vegetable oil

Preheat the oven to 350°F.

Cut each chicken breast piece into thirds, lengthwise, and then crosswise into ¾-inch to 1-inch segments. Put in a bowl. Add the black pepper, turmeric, cayenne pepper, cumin, thyme, garlic powder, paprika, salt, and 1 tablespoon of the oil. Mix well and set aside for 10 minutes or longer.

Heat 2 tablespoons oil in a wok or large, nonstick frying pan over very high heat. When the oil is very hot, put in the chicken. Stir and fry quickly until the chicken pieces are lightly browned or turn opaque on the outside. Put in a baking dish, cover loosely with lightly oiled waxed paper (which should sit inside the dish and directly on the chicken pieces), and bake for 8 to 10 minutes or until the chicken pieces are just cooked through. If not to be eaten immediately, remove the chicken pieces from the hot baking dish to prevent them from drying out.

SERVES 6–8

EASY CHICKEN KEBABS
Murgh tikka

∎∎∎∎∎∎∎

You may serve these kebabs with drinks, as a first course, or even as a light main dish. The pieces of meat may be skewered before being broiled or they may be simply spread out on a broiling tray.

INGREDIENTS

4 boned, skinned chicken breast halves (about 1¼ pounds)	*2 cloves garlic, peeled and crushed to a pulp*
¾ teaspoon salt	*¼ teaspoon cayenne pepper*
2 tablespoons fresh lemon juice	*¼ teaspoon ground turmeric*
3 tablespoons plain yogurt	*½ teaspoon ground cumin*
1 tablespoon chickpea flour (also called gram flour or besan)	*½ teaspoon homemade garam masala (page 134)*
1 teaspoon peeled, very finely grated fresh ginger	*4 tablespoons (½ stick) melted butter or vegetable oil for basting*

Cut each breast half into halves, lengthwise, and then crosswise into 1-inch pieces. Put in a bowl. Rub with ½ teaspoon of the salt and the lemon juice.

Put the yogurt into a separate small bowl. Add the chickpea flour and mix well. Now put in the remaining ¼ teaspoon salt, ginger, garlic, cayenne pepper, turmeric, cumin and *garam masala*. Mix well and pour this mixture over the chicken pieces. Mix well and set aside for 15 minutes or longer (you could even leave it covered in the refrigerator overnight).

Preheat the broiler.

Thread the chicken pieces onto 4 skewers and balance the skewers on the raised edges of a broiling tray. Or you could, as an alternative, spread the chicken pieces out on the broiling tray. Baste with the melted butter or oil. Broil about 4 inches from the heat source for 5 minutes, basting once during this time. Turn the chicken pieces over, baste again, and broil for another 2 to 3 minutes or until the chicken pieces are just cooked through. Serve immediately.

SERVES 4

CHICKEN LIVERS WITH FENNEL AND BLACK PEPPER

Murgh ki masedar kaleji

■ ■ ■ ■ ■ ■

Cook these livers lightly so there is just a hint of pink inside them. You may serve them as a first course or on toast as a snack.

INGREDIENTS

¼ teaspoon ground turmeric	10 fresh curry leaves (page 134) if available
1 teaspoon ground cumin	3 cloves garlic, peeled and finely chopped
1 teaspoon ground coriander	1 pound chicken livers, trimmed and separated into 2 lobes each
¼ teaspoon cayenne pepper	½ teaspoon salt or to taste
1 tablespoon grainy mustard (Pommery *Moutarde de Meaux*, see page 135)	Freshly ground black pepper
	½ cup heavy, whipping cream
3 tablespoons vegetable oil	3 tablespoons finely chopped fresh cilantro (Chinese parsley, fresh green coriander)
¼ teaspoon fennel or aniseed	

Put the turmeric, cumin, coriander, cayenne pepper, and mustard into a small bowl along with 2 tablespoons water. Mix well and set this spice paste aside.

Put the oil in a wok or a frying pan and set over high heat. When hot, put in the fennel seeds, curry leaves, and garlic. Stir and fry until the garlic turns golden. Put in the chicken livers. Sprinkle with ½ teaspoon salt and lots of black pepper. Stir and toss for 3 to 4 minutes or until nicely browned. Remove the livers with a slotted spoon and put in a serving dish or bowl. Put the spice paste into the frying pan. Stir for 15 seconds or so. Put in the cream and a light sprinkling of salt. Stir for 30 to 60 seconds or until the cream is slightly reduced. Pour the sauce over the chicken livers, sprinkle the cilantro over the top, and serve.

SERVES 4–8

SHRIMP WITH GARLIC AND CHILIES

Lehsun vali jhinga

∎∎∎∎∎∎∎

Shrimp cook so fast. The only time you will spend here is in peeling and deveining them. I like to do this ahead of time and then keep them, washed and patted dry, in a plastic bag in the refrigerator, just ready to be stir-fried. They are perfect as a cocktail snack with toothpicks stuck in them, or as a first course. You may serve them as a main dish as well. This recipe will serve six people as a first course or three to four people as a main one.

INGREDIENTS

1 pound medium-sized shrimp, peeled, deveined, and washed (page 131), then patted dry
¼ teaspoon ground turmeric
¼ teaspoon cayenne pepper
¼ cup vegetable oil
½ teaspoon black or yellow mustard seeds

5 cloves garlic, peeled and finely chopped
1 fresh, hot green chili, finely chopped (do not remove seeds)
½ teaspoon salt
2 teaspoons finely chopped fresh cilantro (Chinese parsley, fresh green coriander or parsley)

Put the shrimp in a bowl. Sprinkle the turmeric and cayenne over them evenly and rub in.

Put the oil in a wok or large frying pan and set over high heat. When the oil is very hot, put in the mustard seeds. As soon as they begin to pop—this takes a few seconds—put in the garlic. Stir until the garlic has turned golden. Put in the green chili. Stir once or twice. Put in the shrimp. Stir and fry them over high heat just until they turn opaque. This will take 2 to 3 minutes. Sprinkle with salt and toss. Sprinkle with the cilantro, then toss and serve.

SERVES 6–8

SANDWICHES WITH MINT AND CHILI BUTTER

Pudinay aur mirch ki sandwich

■ ■ ■ ■ ■ ■

No proper Indian tea was ever served without proper English sandwiches, though our idea of "proper" often managed to be something slightly spicy.

INGREDIENTS

6 tablespoons unsalted butter, softened
1 teaspoon fresh lemon juice
10 fresh mint leaves, finely chopped
½ to 1 fresh, hot green chili, finely chopped
(do not remove seeds)

A generous pinch salt
Freshly ground black pepper
10 thin slices sandwich bread
3 to 4 lettuce leaves, washed, dried, and cut into fine, long slivers

In a small bowl, combine the butter, lemon juice, mint, green chili, salt, and black pepper. Mix well. Using this mixture, butter each slice of bread generously on one side. Put 2 slices together, buttered sides meeting each other. Cut off the crusts and then cut the sandwiches in halves, diagonally. Spread most of the lettuce on a serving plate. Arrange the sandwiches on top. Scatter a few of the lettuce shreds over the sandwiches and serve.

SERVES 10

ONION FRITTERS

Pyaz ki bhajia

∎∎∎∎∎∎

Even though these fritters are served as a first course in many restaurants—and there is no reason why they should not be—in India they are generally served as a snack with tea. They may also be served with drinks. This particular recipe, in which an egg is used in the batter, comes from my friend, Badi Uzzaman, who played the part of my husband in the British television series *Firm Friends*.

Fresh Green Chutney (page 113) should be served on the side.

INGREDIENTS

1 large egg	¼ teaspoon ground turmeric
1 tablespoon fresh lemon juice	1 fresh, hot green chili, finely chopped (do not remove seeds)
1 cup chickpea flour (also called gram flour or besan)	2 tablespoons chopped fresh cilantro (Chinese parsley, fresh green coriander)
¾ teaspoon salt	Vegetable oil for deep-frying
½ teaspoon cayenne pepper	1 medium-large onion (about 7 ounces), peeled and chopped into medium-sized dice
½ teaspoon store-bought garam masala (page 134)	
½ teaspoon cumin seeds	
1 teaspoon ground cumin	

Break the egg into a bowl and beat well. Add the water and the lemon juice. Mix. Add all the chickpea flour and mix well with a whisk. Put in the salt, cayenne pepper, *garam masala,* cumin seeds, ground cumin, turmeric, green chili, and cilantro. Mix well and set aside for at least 10 minutes. Mix again with a whisk. The batter should be of a droppable consistency.

Put the oil for deep-frying in a wok or deep fryer and set over medium heat. You should have at least 3 inches oil in the center of the wok. When the oil is hot, put the onion into the batter and mix. (This should always be done just before frying.) Remove heaping teaspoons of the batter and drop it into the hot oil. Use up all the batter this way. Stir and fry the fritters for 7 to 8 minutes or until they are a golden red. Remove the fritters with a slotted spoon and drain on a plate lined with paper towels. Serve hot, as soon as the fritters are made.

SERVES 6

CHICKPEAS COOKED IN TEA

Dhabay kay chanay

■ ■ ■ ■ ■ ■ ■

Cooked in tea? You might well ask! This is the trick that all the vendors at truck stops use to give their chickpeas a traditional dark appearance. The tea—leftover tea may be used here—leaves no aftertaste. It just alters the color of the chickpeas.

For speed, I have used canned chickpeas. As they are already cooked, they need just 10 minutes of gentle simmering to absorb the flavorings. I have also used canned chopped tomatoes. If you wish to substitute fresh, chop them very finely and use ½ cup instead of ¼ cup.

This chickpea dish may be served with store-bought pita bread, a yogurt relish, and some pickles or salad. It could also be served as a snack or as part of a more elaborate meal with meat or chicken, a green vegetable, and rice.

INGREDIENTS

2 cans (19 ounces each) chickpeas (garbanzo beans)	1 to 2 fresh, hot green chilies, cut into very fine rounds (do not remove seeds)
¼ cup vegetable oil	
Generous pinch ground asafetida (page 132), optional	1 teaspoon salt
1 teaspoon cumin seeds	2 teaspoons ground toasted cumin seeds (page 133)
1 medium-small onion (6 ounces), peeled and chopped	1 teaspoon store-bought garam masala (page 134)
3 cloves garlic, peeled and finely chopped	3 to 4 tablespoons coarsely fresh cilantro (Chinese parsley, fresh green coriander)
¼ cup canned chopped tomatoes	
2 teaspoons peeled, finely grated ginger	1 tablespoon fresh lemon juice
1¼ cups prepared tea (use a plain black tea; water may be substituted)	

Drain the chickpeas. Rinse them gently with fresh water. Drain again.

Put the oil in a wide pan and set over medium-high heat. When the oil is hot, put in the *asafetida*. Let it sizzle for a second. Now put in the cumin seeds and let them sizzle for about 15 seconds. Put in the onion. Stir and fry until the onion turns quite brown at the edges. Put in the garlic and let it turn golden, stirring as this happens. Now put in the tomatoes. Stir and cook them until they turn dark and thick. Add the ginger and give a few good stirs. Now put in the chickpeas and all the remaining ingredients. Bring to a simmer. Turn the heat to low and simmer, uncovered, for about 10 minutes, stirring gently now and then. Taste for balance of flavors and make necessary adjustments.

SERVES 4–5

BEEF, LAMB, AND PORK

■ ■ ■ ■ ■ ■ ■

Apart from quick kebabs and stir-fries such as *jhal firezi* (page 37) most Indian meat dishes are stewed. Stewed slowly. So this was, potentially, the hardest chapter for me to put together. I knew I could use a pressure cooker. Most of my Indian relatives do. But I had always hated pressure cookers. The one I had hissed threateningly and was impossible to open once it had been shut. I always had to call out to my husband to come and pry the lid away from the pot. Also, its shape was all wrong. I like wide pots that allow me to stir and brown the meat.

Just about the time I started working on this book, I heard about a pressure cooker made by the Kuhn-Rikon company in Switzerland (see page 129) and ordered one that had the shape of a deep frying pan. I fell in love with it. (You can read more about it at the back of the book.) It worked magically and, what is more, had a stainless steel bottom that seemed to have the qualities of a nonstick one. I was sold.

I have selected dishes for this chapter that do not require time spent browning spice pastes, a task specially invented by some malevolent god to teach Indians patience. In these recipes everything tends to get thrown into the pot at once and any browning that is done is done at the end—which is much easier, as it almost happens by itself.

■ ■ ■ ■ ■ ■ ■

■ ■ ■ ■ ■ ■ ■

■ ■ ■ ■ ■ ■ ■

GROUND LAMB WITH TOMATOES AND PEAS

Keema matar

■■■■■■■

The quickest method of chopping onion, garlic, and ginger finely is to put them into a food processor and use the "pulse" method: rapidly start and stop the machine until you have the result you want. That is what I have done here. Of course, you could also use a chef's knife.

INGREDIENTS

1 small onion (about 4 ounces), peeled and coarsely chopped	*¼ cup plain yogurt*
2-inch piece fresh ginger, peeled and coarsely chopped	*1¼ pounds ground lamb*
5 to 6 large cloves garlic, peeled and coarsely chopped	*1¼ teaspoons salt*
¼ cup vegetable oil	*2 teaspoons store-bought* garam masala *(page 134)*
½ teaspoon cayenne pepper	*2 tablespoons fresh lemon juice*
1 teaspoon cumin seeds	*1 fresh, hot green chili, chopped (do not remove seeds)*
1 teaspoon coriander seeds	*6 tablespoons coarsely chopped fresh cilantro (Chinese parsley, fresh green coriander)*
½ teaspoon ground turmeric	
1 medium-sized tomato (about 7 ounces), chopped	*1 cup peas, fresh or frozen*

Put the onion, ginger, and garlic into the container of a food processor and chop finely.

Put the oil in a wide, nonstick pan and set over medium-high heat. When the oil is hot, put in the finely chopped onion, ginger, and garlic mixture. Stir and fry until it is somewhat brown. Put in the cayenne, cumin seeds, coriander seeds, and turmeric. Stir once or twice. Now put in the tomato and yogurt. Stir on high heat until the tomato is soft. Put in the meat, salt, and *garam masala*. Stir, breaking up any lumps, for 2 minutes. Put in 1 cup water. Stir and bring to a simmer. Cover and turn the heat to low and simmer for 25 minutes. Add the lemon juice, green chili, cilantro, and peas. Stir and bring back to a simmer. Cover and cook on low heat for 10 minutes.

SERVES 4–6

"HAMBURGER" KEBABS

Chappal kebab

■ ■ ■ ■ ■ ■

Forgive this long preamble. Let me say at the very start that these kebabs are utterly delicious and can be prepared—from start to finish—in as few as 15 minutes. Now let me tell you a story.

One of my very good Indian friends—I always call her a hill woman, as she is from the mountainous Himalayan region—was convalescing in bed in New York, recovering from an operation. I had taken some of the season's freshest cherries to cheer her up. She was duly grateful, but as we talked and she nibbled on the cherries, I realized that her mind was on something else. Did I know of any restaurants that served *chappali kebabs?* I did not know, nor had I heard of these kebabs. Well, she suggested, they were a real treat and I should go with her husband right away, have some kebabs at this restaurant, and then bring some back for her as well. She gave us an address. It turned out to be the address of the wrong restaurant. Her husband and I ate some rather pitiful kebabs and, what is more, he took back four orders to please his bedridden wife.

All this started me off on a quest, the first part of which was to find the right place, which my friend now remembered. The other part was to get the recipe from the owners. The right place was hard enough to find, as it was in the very seedy Times Square district of New York, had no sign outside, and looked like a video shop—which it was. But once I had found it and managed to taste the wonderful kebabs, getting the recipe was even harder. The owner kept saying that these kebabs, which were really like thin, spicy, and utterly mouthwatering hamburgers, were made of "meat and spices" and that they were a specialty of the Pakistani city of Peshawar.

So I did the next best thing. I bought half a dozen kebabs, took them to the car where my husband waited, and then dissected and analyzed them as we gobbled them up. I think I have got it! And here it is.

These kebabs are meant to be very spicy. I have used just two green chilies but you could use one whole chili per kebab if you are up to it. They may be eaten with rice and vegetables but are best cut in half and rolled up in a flat bread—such as *chapati* or *naan* or store-bought pita—along with a little salad and either some Fresh Green Chutney (page 113) or Fresh Red Chutney with Almonds (page 114). You could also eat them like a hamburger, in a hamburger bun. Again, a little salad and fresh chutney should be sandwiched in as well.

Small versions of these kebabs may be served with drinks.

1 tablespoon chickpea flour (also called gram flour or besan)
1½ pounds ground beef or lamb put three times through the grinder; it should be quite fine—the butcher could do this
6 to 7 tablespoons coarsely chopped fresh cilantro (Chinese parsley, fresh green coriander)
2 or more fresh, hot green chilies, cut into fine rounds and chopped (do not remove seeds)

1½ teaspoons cumin seeds
1½ teaspoons coriander seeds
1 teaspoon freshly ground black pepper
1¼ teaspoons salt
½ lightly beaten egg
3 to 4 tablespoons vegetable oil

Put the chickpea flour in a small cast-iron frying pan and stir around over medium heat until the flour has turned a light brown color. Put it into a bowl. Add all the other ingredients except the oil and mix well. Form ten 2-inch balls. Flatten the balls to make ten 3½-inch hamburgerlike patties.

Just before eating, put 2 tablespoons of the oil into a large nonstick frying pan and set over medium-high heat. When the oil is hot, put in as many kebabs as the pan will hold in a single layer. Turning them over every 20 seconds or so, cook the kebabs for about 2½ minutes or until they have browned on both sides. Removed to a warm plate. Use the remaining oil to cook a second batch the same way.

SERVES 4–5

THE MOST DELICIOUS MEAT CUBES

Boti gosht

■■■■■■

This is, quite simply, an exquisite dish. It has no sauce. The meat cubes are almost like kebabs, except that they are cooked in a saucepan. I have used a pressure cooker to speed up things, but you could use an ordinary saucepan. Add about ¾ cup water, cover the pan, and cook gently for about 50 minutes before uncovering and boiling down the liquid.

In India, this is made with goat meat. In the West, I tend to make it with boned pork shoulder cut into kebablike cubes. Boned shoulder of lamb would work as well.

You could serve it as part of an Indian meal with Indian breads or rice or with Indian Mashed Potatoes (page 90) and Simply Grilled Tomatoes (page 93), or, for an even easier meal, with plain boiled potatoes and a green salad.

INGREDIENTS

3 tablespoons vegetable oil
1½-inch piece fresh ginger, peeled and very finely chopped
4 cloves garlic, peeled and very finely chopped
15 fresh or dried curry leaves (page 134), if available
1 pound boned shoulder of lamb or pork, cut into 1-inch cubes
2 teaspoons store-bought garam masala *(page 134)*
1 teaspoon ground cumin

¼ teaspoon ground turmeric
¼ teaspoon cayenne pepper
1 fresh, hot green chili, finely sliced (do not remove seeds)
½ teaspoon salt or to taste
Freshly ground black pepper
1½ to 2 teaspoons fresh lemon juice

Put the oil in a pressure cooker and set over medium-high heat. When the oil is hot, put in the ginger, garlic, and curry leaves. Stir. When the garlic starts to brown, put in the meat. Stir once or twice and turn the heat to medium-low. Now put in the *garam masala*, cumin, turmeric, cayenne pepper, green chili, and salt. Stir to mix. Add 2 tablespoons water and cover tightly. Turn the heat to high and bring up to pressure. Lower the heat and cook under pressure for 15 minutes. Remove from the heat and reduce the pressure quickly with the help of cool water poured on the lid. Remove the cover. Cook, uncovered, over high heat until all the liquid has gone and the meat has browned a bit. Stir as you do this. Stir in lots of freshly ground black pepper and the lemon juice.

SERVES 3–4

LAMB WITH CARDAMOM

Elaichi gosht

■■■■■■

Many versions of this dish exist among the Sindhi community of India. This recipe comes from Draupadiji, a veritable treasure-house of Sindhi specialties.

Here the green cardamom pods are ground whole, husks and all. This may be done in a clean coffee grinder or other spice grinder, or even in a good-quality blender.

This mild, aromatic dish—it has no red chilies but plenty of black pepper—is very much like a stew: gentle and soothing. It should have quite a bit of sauce. Sindhis often eat it with bread, so serving it with a good, crusty Italian or French loaf would be downright authentic. You may serve a salad or a selection of Indian vegetables on the side.

You do not, of course, have to use a pressure cooker here. If you use an ordinary saucepan, put in 2½ cups water and cook for 1 hour or a bit longer.

INGREDIENTS

2 tablespoons cardamom pods (the green kind sold by Indian grocers are best)
3 tablespoons vegetable oil
2 pounds boned shoulder of lamb, cut into 1-inch cubes
2 large tomatoes, chopped
¼ cup finely chopped onions (red onions or shallots are ideal but any onions will do)

1½ teaspoon store-bought garam masala *(page 134)*
1 tablespoon tomato paste
1½ teaspoons salt or to taste
Lots of freshly ground black pepper

Put the cardamom pods into the container of a clean coffee grinder or other spice grinder and grind them until you have a fine powder.

Put the oil in a pressure cooker and set over medium-high heat. When the oil is hot, put in the cardamom powder. Stir once and put in all the meat. Stir over high heat for 2 minutes. Put in the tomatoes and onions. Stir for another 3 minutes. Now put in the *garam masala*, tomato paste, salt, and 2 cups water. Cover tightly and bring up to pressure. Turn the heat to low and cook for 15 minutes. Reduce the pressure quickly with cool water and uncover. Heat the meat again over high heat. Grind in a very generous amount of black pepper and cook, stirring gently, for a minute. Check the salt.

SERVES 6

SMOTHERED LAMB (OR PORK OR BEEF)

Labdhara gosht

■ ■ ■ ■ ■ ■ ■

There may be a fair number of ingredients in this dish but as they all go into the pan at almost the same time, the preparation is quite painless. The taste, however, is scrumptious.

If you do not wish to use a pressure cooker, this dish may just as easily be cooked in a regular saucepan. It will take anywhere from 1 to 1½ hours (the longer time for beef) and you will need to add about ½ cup water just before you begin the simmering.

INGREDIENTS

1 pound boned shoulder of lamb or pork or stewing beef, cut into 1-inch cubes

1 small onion (about 4 ounces), peeled and finely chopped

1-inch piece fresh ginger, peeled and finely chopped

1 medium-sized tomato (about 5 ounces), peeled and finely chopped

About ½ cup finely chopped cilantro (Chinese parsley, fresh green coriander)

1 to 2 fresh, hot green chilies, cut into fine rings (do not remove seeds)

¼ teaspoon ground turmeric

2 teaspoons store-bought garam masala (page 134)

1 teaspoon ground cumin

¼ cup plain yogurt

1 tablespoon tomato paste

¾ teaspoon salt or to taste

3 tablespoons vegetable oil

4 cloves garlic, peeled and finely chopped

Freshly ground black pepper

Put all the ingredients except the oil, garlic, and black pepper into a bowl and mix well.

Put the oil in a pressure cooker and set over medium-high heat. When the oil is hot, put in the garlic. Stir until the garlic pieces turn medium brown. Now put in the seasoned meat and stir once or twice. Turn the heat to medium. Cover the pressure cooker tightly and bring up to pressure slowly. Cook lamb and pork for 15 minutes and beef for 20 minutes at full pressure. Reduce the pressure quickly with the help of cool water poured on the lid. Uncover. Cook, uncovered, over high heat until the sauce is thick, stirring gently as you do so. Sprinkle in lots of black pepper and stir again.

SERVES 3–4

LAMB WITH ONIONS

Kaliya

∎∎∎∎∎∎∎

This is a very simple way to prepare a traditional dish—everything goes into the pressure cooker together and a lot of fuss is avoided! If you wish to use an ordinary saucepan, increase the juice from the canned tomato to 1½ to 1¾ cups (water may be used too). Cook for 50 to 60 minutes before taking off the lid and reducing the liquid.

INGREDIENTS

3 tablespoons vegetable oil

2 small onions (about 9 ounces in all), peeled and cut into fine half rings

1-inch piece fresh ginger, peeled and cut into fine slivers

6 cloves garlic, peeled and finely chopped

1½ pounds boned shoulder of lamb, cut into 1½-inch chunks

2 to 6 fresh, hot green chilies, sliced into rounds (do not remove seeds)

2 canned plum tomatoes, coarsely chopped, and 6 tablespoons of juice from the can

6 tablespoons plain yogurt

1 teaspoon ground roasted cumin seeds (page 133)

1 teaspoon salt

1 teaspoon homemade garam masala *(page 134)*

Put all the ingredients except the *garam masala* into a pressure cooker and mix well. Turn the heat to medium and secure the top of the pressure cooker. Leave on medium heat for 5 minutes and then turn the heat up to high and build up the pressure. When the pressure is fully up, turn the heat to low and cook for 15 minutes. Reduce the pressure quickly with the help of cool water poured on the lid and open the pot. Add the *garam masala* and cook, uncovered, over high heat for about 10 minutes or until the sauce is thick and greatly reduced. Stir gently as you do this.

SERVES 4

PORK OR LAMB VINDALOO
Vindaloo

∎∎∎∎∎∎

The essential ingredients for this Portuguese-inspired Indian dish are wine vinegar and garlic. Additions of mustard seeds, cumin, turmeric, and chilies make it specifically colonial Goan.

Most recipes for *vindaloo* involve grinding mustard seeds in vinegar. To save this step, I have used grainy French mustard (Pommery *Moutarde de Meaux*), which already contains vinegar. It works beautifully.

This dish may be made in the pressure cooker (20 minutes of simmering time) or in a frying pan (1 hour or so of simmering). Either way, once the simmering starts, the cook can read a book, sleep, or have a drink! It is painless cooking.

Vindaloos are hot. Goans would use 4 teaspoons of cayenne here. Under my husband's "spare-me" gaze, I have used half a teaspoon to make a mild dish. It is up to you.

INGREDIENTS

1½ tablespoons grainy mustard (Pommery *Moutarde de Meaux*)	3 tablespoons vegetable oil
1½ teaspoons ground cumin	1 small onion (about 4 ounces), peeled and cut into fine half rings
¾ teaspoons ground turmeric	6 large cloves garlic, peeled and crushed to a pulp
½ to 1 teaspoon cayenne pepper	1¼ pounds boned shoulder of pork or lamb, cut into 1-inch cubes
1 teaspoon salt	⅔ cup canned coconut milk, well stirred
1 teaspoon red wine vinegar	

Combine the mustard, cumin, turmeric, cayenne, salt, and vinegar in a cup. Mix well.

Put the oil in a large, nonstick frying pan and set over medium-high heat. When the oil is hot, put in the onion. Stir and fry until is it medium brown. Put in the garlic. Stir and fry for 30 seconds. Put in the spice paste. Stir and fry for a minute. Put in the meat. Stir and fry for about 3 minutes. Now add the coconut milk and ⅔ cup water if you are going to cook in a pressure cooker or 1 cup water if you are going to continue to cook in the frying pan. (Transfer to a pressure cooker at this stage if that is your intention.) Cover and either bring up to pressure, or bring to a boil if you are using the frying pan. Lower the heat to a simmer and cook for 20 minutes in the pressure cooker and 60 to 70 minutes in the frying pan.

SERVES 3–4

LAMB STEWED IN COCONUT MILK

Safed gosht

■■■■■■

This is a meal in itself, an Indian meat-and-potato casserole that requires only rice—or a good crusty bread, if you like—on the side. I always serve something green as well, such as Stir-Fried Green Cabbage with Fennel Seeds (page 88), but a simple green salad would be equally good.

I have used a pressure cooker for speed. The cooking time in a saucepan would be about 70 minutes and you would need to add about ¾ cup water before starting to cook. This stew may be made up to a day ahead and reheated.

INGREDIENTS

3 tablespoons vegetable oil

12 fresh curry leaves (page 134) if available, or 3 bay leaves

2-inch stick cinnamon

6 cardamom pods

8 whole cloves

15 black peppercorns

About ⅓ cup (3 ounces) peeled and chopped onion

1½ pounds boned shoulder of lamb, cut into 1½-inch chunks

1 pound potatoes, peeled and cut into pieces the same size as the meat

2 medium-sized carrots, peeled and cut into 3 pieces each

¼ teaspoon ground turmeric

1 tablespoon ground coriander

⅛ to ½ teaspoon cayenne pepper

1 to 2 fresh, hot green chilies

1¼ teaspoon salt

1 can (14 ounces) coconut milk, well stirred

Put the oil in a pressure cooker and set over medium-high heat. When the oil is hot, put in the curry leaves (if using), cinnamon, cardamom, cloves, and peppercorns. Stir once and put in the onion. Sauté for 1½ minutes or until the onion is soft, and put in the meat, potatoes, carrots, turmeric, coriander, cayenne, green chilies, salt, and 1 cup of the well-stirred coconut milk. Cover securely with the lid and, on high heat, bring up to full pressure. Turn the heat to low and cook for 15 minutes. Lower the pressure with the help of cool water poured on the lid and remove the lid. Cook, uncovered, over high heat for 5 to 6 minutes, stirring gently as you do this. Add the remaining coconut milk and bring to a simmer. Turn off the heat.

SERVES 4

BEEF OR LAMB WITH SPINACH

Saag gosht

■ ■ ■ ■ ■ ■

This is the classic dish, prepared in almost every north Indian home and loved by all. To make it quickly, a pressure cooker is essential. If you use a regular saucepan, it will take about 1 hour for the lamb to cook and 1½ hours for beef. You will need to increase the amount of water to 2½ cups. It helps to have a food processor to chop the onion, ginger, and garlic finely at great speed.

INGREDIENTS

1 package (10 ounces) frozen chopped spinach	Two 2-inch sticks cinnamon
1 large onion (about 10 ounces) peeled and coarsely chopped	1⅓ pounds stewing beef or boned shoulder of lamb, cut into 1 ½-inch pieces
2-inch piece fresh ginger, peeled and coarsely chopped	1⅓ teaspoons salt
6 to 8 cloves garlic, peeled	1 tablespoon ground coriander
6 tablespoons vegetable oil	1 teaspoon ground cumin
3 bay leaves	¼ to 1 teaspoon cayenne pepper
10 cardamom pods	½ teaspoon homemade or store-bought garam masala *(page 134)*
8 whole cloves	

Following the instructions on the package, drop the spinach into boiling water and boil just until it is defrosted. Drain and squeeze out most of the water.

Put the onion, ginger, and garlic into the container of a food processor and pulse, starting and stopping with great rapidity until finely chopped.

Put the oil in a pressure cooker and set over high heat. When the oil is hot, put in the bay leaves, cardamom pods, cloves and cinnamon sticks. Stir once or twice and put in the finely chopped onion, ginger, and garlic. Stir and cook over high heat for 5 minutes. Put in the beef or lamb, the spinach, 2 cups water, salt, coriander, cumin, and cayenne. Stir. Cover, securing the pressure cooker lid, and bring up to full pressure over high heat. Now lower the heat and cook at full pressure. The beef will take 20 minutes, the lamb 15 minutes. Cool off the pressure cooker quickly with cool water on the lid and remove the lid. Put in the *garam masala* and bring the contents of the pressure cooker to a boil again. Cook, uncovered, stirring gently over high heat for 7 to 10 minutes or until the sauce is reduced and thick. (When serving, leave the oil behind.)

SERVES 4

BEEF OR LAMB WITH ONION AND GREEN PEPPER

Jhal firezi

■■■■■■■

An Anglo-Indian specialty, this calls for leftovers of cooked roast beef or roast lamb. Sunday's roast was invariably turned into a delicious *jhal firezi* on Mondays by many a family in cities such as Calcutta.

One or two sliced green chilies may be added to this dish at the same time as the green bell pepper if you want it really hot. It is worth noting that the use of Worcestershire sauce in cooking is fairly typical of Anglo-Indian households.

You may serve this dish with rice, potatoes, or breads. The meat is also excellent stuffed into pita breads with some shredded lettuce and sliced tomato.

INGREDIENTS

12 ounces cooked, boneless roast beef or roast lamb	3 tablespoons vegetable oil
½ teaspoon freshly ground black pepper	½ teaspoon cumin seeds
¼ to ½ teaspoon cayenne pepper	½ teaspoon black or yellow mustard seeds
1 teaspoon ground cumin	10 fenugreek seeds (optional)
1 teaspoon ground coriander	1 small green bell pepper (about 4 ounces), de-seeded and cut,
¼ teaspoon ground turmeric	lengthwise, into ⅛-inch slivers
1 teaspoon red wine vinegar	1 small onion (about 4 ounces), peeled and cut into fine half rings
½ plus ⅛ teaspoon salt	1 teaspoon Worcestershire sauce

Cut the cooked meat into ¼-inch-wide slices. Now stack a few slices together at a time and cut them into ¼-inch slivers. This does not have to be done too evenly.

Combine the black pepper, cayenne, ground cumin, ground coriander, turmeric, vinegar, ½ teaspoon salt, and 2 tablespoons water in a small cup. Mix and set aside.

Put the oil in a large frying pan over medium-high heat. When the oil is hot, put in the cumin, mustard, and optional fenugreek seeds. As soon as the mustard seeds begin to pop, put in the green bell pepper and onion. Stir and fry until the onion has browned quite a bit and the mass of vegetables has reduced. Sprinkle about ⅛ teaspoon salt over the top and stir. Add the meat and the spice mixture from the cup. Stir rapidly on the same medium-high heat for a minute or so until the meat has heated through. Add the Worcestershire sauce and stir to mix.

SERVES 3–4

EGGS AND POULTRY

■ ■ ■ ■ ■ ■ ■

When I was growing up, chicken was considered special. It was really party food, but the family could have it on, say, a Saturday evening as a special treat. For me, its aura still remains, even though it is now cheap and easily available. This aura is probably connected with the way chicken was cooked. Because it was not an everyday food, it was prepared in a more interesting manner. Here follow some of the recipes from my childhood. All I have done is simplify the techniques to lessen your exertion. The tastes remain the same.

■ ■ ■ ■ ■ ■ ■

....

....

HARD-BOILED EGGS MASALA

Masaledar ublay unday

∎ ∎ ∎ ∎ ∎ ∎

This can be whipped up quickly for lunch or supper. The eggs may be served with rice or even bread (toasted or plain).

INGREDIENTS

½ teaspoon cayenne pepper

½ teaspoon ground turmeric

1 teaspoon ground cumin

1 teaspoon ground coriander

1 teaspoon fresh lemon juice

¾ teaspoon salt

Freshly ground black pepper

2 tablespoons vegetable oil

½ teaspoon cumin seeds

5 tablespoons (2½ ounces) peeled and finely chopped onion

½-inch piece fresh ginger, peeled and finely chopped

1 cup canned chopped tomatoes (or lightly drained, canned whole tomatoes, finely chopped)

¼ teaspoon sugar

3 to 4 tablespoons chopped fresh cilantro (Chinese parsley, fresh green coriander)

4 hard-boiled eggs, peeled and cut into halves lengthwise

Combine the cayenne, turmeric, ground cumin, ground coriander, lemon juice, salt, black pepper, and 1 tablespoon water in a small bowl. Mix.

Put the oil in a medium-sized, nonstick frying pan and set over medium-high heat. When the oil is hot, put in the cumin seeds. Ten seconds later, put in the onion and ginger. Stir and fry until the onion turns medium brown. Put in the spice paste. Stir and cook for 15 seconds. Now put in the tomatoes and sugar. Bring to a simmer. Cover and simmer gently for 10 minutes. Put in the cilantro. Stir once or twice. Lay the cut eggs in the sauce and spoon more sauce over them. Cover and simmer gently for 2 to 3 minutes.

SERVES 2–4

GARLICKY MUSHROOM MASALA OMELET

Masala omlate

∎∎∎∎∎∎∎

This is an ideal dish for a brunch, a light lunch, or even a quick light supper. You may serve it with toast and tea, as in Indian hotels, or with crusty French bread, a green salad, and perhaps some cool white wine.

The chopped tomatoes are straight out of a can. You may substitute canned whole tomatoes that have been lightly drained and finely chopped or, in season, use double the quantity of very finely chopped fresh tomatoes. You don't need to peel them.

INGREDIENTS

5 large eggs
Salt as needed
Freshly ground black pepper
¼ cup vegetable oil
½ teaspoon black or yellow mustard seeds
1 large clove garlic, peeled and very finely chopped
4 large or 6 medium-sized mushrooms, sliced lengthwise
3 scallions (green onions), cut into very fine rounds (the white as well as the green part)

1 fresh, hot green chili, cut into very fine rounds (do not remove seeds)
4 heaping tablespoons coarsely chopped fresh cilantro (Chinese parsley, fresh green coriander)
½ teaspoon peeled, finely grated fresh ginger
¼ cup canned chopped tomatoes (for variations, see recipe introduction)

Break the eggs into a bowl. Add a generous ¼ teaspoon salt and some freshly ground black pepper and beat well. Pour into a glass measuring cup.

Put 2 tablespoons of the oil in a medium-sized frying pan and set over high heat. When the oil is hot, put in the mustard seeds. As soon as they begin to pop—this takes just a few seconds—put in the garlic. Stir once or twice. As soon as the garlic starts to brown, put in the mushrooms and stir until the mushrooms lose their raw look. Now turn the heat to medium and put in the scallions, green chili, cilantro, and ginger. Stir until the green seasonings have wilted—about a minute. Put in the tomatoes and a little salt and pepper. Stir for about 30 seconds (or, for fresh tomatoes, until they are no longer watery) and turn off the heat. This is the filling.

Put 1 tablespoon of the oil in a 7-inch nonstick frying pan or omelet pan and set over high heat. When hot, pour in half the beaten eggs. Using a wooden spoon or the back of a fork, stir the eggs for the next 3 to 4 seconds until they look like lumps of soft custard held together in one unbroken layer. Quickly spread half the stuffing along the center of the omelet and fold it over. Cook for another few seconds and flip the omelet over onto a warm plate. Make the second one the same way.

SERVES 2

EGGS WITH FRESH GREEN HERBS

Hare masale ka omlate

■ ■ ■ ■ ■ ■

This may be served at breakfast and brunch as soon as it comes out of the frying pan (I serve it with toast) and may also be sliced and put onto sandwiches to perk up a picnic or an office lunch. It is really a flat egg pancake seasoned with scallions, cilantro, green chilies, ginger, and garlic.

It is a good idea to have everything cut and ready before you start, as this dish cooks very quickly.

INGREDIENTS

5 large eggs

¼ plus ⅓ teaspoon salt

Freshly ground black pepper

2 tablespoons vegetable oil

3 scallions (green onions), cut into fine rounds (the white as well as the green sections)

¼ teaspoon peeled, very finely chopped garlic

3 tablespoons finely chopped fresh cilantro (Chinese parsley, fresh green coriander)

1 to 3 fresh, hot green chilies, sliced into fine rounds (do not remove seeds)

½ teaspoon peeled, very finely chopped fresh ginger

Generous pinch ground turmeric

1½ teaspoons fresh lemon juice

Break the eggs into a bowl and beat well. Add a generous ¼ teaspoon salt and lots of freshly ground black pepper.

Put the oil into a large, nonstick frying pan and set over medium-high heat. When the oil is hot, put in the scallions. Stir and fry until they just start to brown at the edges. Put in the garlic and stir for a few seconds. Now put in the cilantro, chilies, ginger, and turmeric. Stir for a few seconds. Add the lemon juice and ⅓ teaspoon salt and stir to mix. Working quickly, spread the ingredients evenly in the pan. Now pour in the beaten eggs and let them spread to the edges of the pan. Cover, turn the heat to medium-low, and cook for a few minutes, just until the eggs have set. Cut into wedges and serve immediately.

SERVES 2–4

QUICK CHICKEN KORMA

Murgh korma

■■■■■■■

When trying to cook fast, it helps to have all the right tools and utensils at hand. Here, a blender to make the ginger-garlic paste and a frying pan or sauté pan wide enough to hold all the chicken in a single layer will be of great help. This entire dish can be made a day ahead of time, covered, and refrigerated. It reheats well.

INGREDIENTS

1½-inch piece fresh ginger, peeled and coarsely chopped	*1 small onion (4½ ounces), peeled and finely chopped*
5 to 6 cloves garlic, peeled and coarsely chopped	*1 tablespoon ground coriander*
6 tablespoons vegetable oil	*1 tablespoon ground cumin*
3 bay leaves	*3 canned plum tomatoes, chopped*
2-inch stick cinnamon	*3 pounds chicken pieces, skinned and cut into serving portions*
8 cardamom pods	*¼ to 1 teaspoon cayenne pepper*
4 whole cloves	*¾ teaspoon salt*
¼ teaspoon black cumin seeds (page 134) or ordinary cumin seeds	*3 tablespoons heavy, whipping cream*

Put the ginger, garlic, and 3 tablespoons water in the container of an electric blender. Blend until you have a smooth paste.

Put the oil in a wide frying pan or sauté pan and set over high heat. When the oil is very hot, put in the bay leaves, cinnamon, cardamom pods, cloves, and cumin seeds. Stir once or twice and put in the onion. Stir and fry for about 3 minutes or until the onion turns brownish. Put in the paste from the blender, and the ground coriander and ground cumin and fry for a minute. Put in the chopped tomatoes and fry for another minute. Put in the chicken, cayenne, salt, and 1 cup water. Bring to a boil. Cover, turn the heat to medium and cook for 15 minutes, turning the chicken pieces over now and then. Remove the cover, add the cream, and cook on high heat for another 7 to 8 minutes or until the sauce has thickened. Stir gently as you do this.

SERVES 4

SILKEN CHICKEN

Reshmi murgh

■ ■ ■ ■ ■ ■

The texture of the chicken here is really soft and silken. As this dish takes just 15 minutes to cook and is best eaten fresh out of the oven, I leave it in its marinade until exactly 15 minutes before we sit down to eat. (It can stay in the marinade, covered and refrigerated, for several hours, even overnight, if you like.) Sprinkle the extra spices on just before the chicken goes into the oven.

These chicken breasts may be served Indian-style with rice and vegetables or Western-style with boiled potatoes and either steamed vegetables or a salad. Both would make for light meals. Leftovers, if there are any, can be covered and refrigerated. The chicken is excellent sliced and put into sandwiches or salads.

INGREDIENTS

For Marinating the Chicken	*For Sprinkling over the Chicken*
4 boned, skinned chicken breast halves (about 1¼ pounds)	Salt as needed
½ teaspoon salt	Freshly ground black pepper
2 tablespoons fresh lemon juice	A little homemade garam masala *(page 134)*
¼ cup heavy, whipping cream	A little ground roasted cumin seed *(page 133)*
½ teaspoon homemade garam masala *(page 134)*	A little cayenne pepper
¼ teaspoon cayenne pepper	1 teaspoon dried mint flakes
¼ teaspoon ground roasted cumin seeds *(page 133)*	Generous squeezes of fresh lemon juice
½ teaspoon paprika	
1 clove garlic, peeled and crushed to a pulp	
½ teaspoon peeled, finely grated fresh ginger	

Preheat the oven to its highest temperature and arrange a shelf in the top third of the oven.

Cut 3 diagonal slits across the top of each piece of chicken breast, being careful not to go all the way through and also not to go to the edge. Prick the chicken pieces with the sharp point of a small knife. Place them in a single layer in a large baking dish and rub both sides with the salt and lemon juice. Leave for 5 minutes. Meanwhile, combine the cream with the *garam masala,* cayenne, ground roasted cumin seeds, paprika, garlic, and ginger in a bowl. Stir this mixture well and pour it over the chicken. Rub it into the meat and leave for 10 minutes.

Lift the chicken pieces up—most of the marinade will cling to them—and place them down in a single layer in a shallow baking pan lined with aluminum foil. On top of each, sprinkle a little salt, black pepper, *garam masala,* ground roasted cumin seed, cayenne, dried mint, and lemon juice. Put into the top third of the oven and bake for 15 minutes or until the chicken is just white all the way through. Serve immediately, minted side up.

SERVES 2–4

GROUND CHICKEN OR TURKEY WITH PEAS
Murghi ka keema

■■■■■■■

Ground chicken—or turkey, for that matter—cooks up in minutes. If a guest unexpectedly shows up, this may be the perfect dish to serve. I have used peas here but infinite variations are possible: cooked lima beans, cut-up and cooked green beans, even corn kernels.

INGREDIENTS

3 tablespoons vegetable oil
1-inch stick cinnamon
4 cardamom pods
2 bay leaves
1 small onion (about 4 ounces), peeled and chopped
3 cloves garlic, peeled and finely chopped
2 teaspoons peeled, finely grated fresh ginger
1¼ pounds ground chicken or turkey

6 to 7 ounces fresh or frozen peas, lightly cooked
¼ teaspoon ground turmeric
1 teaspoon store-bought garam masala (page 134)
¼ teaspoon cayenne pepper
½ to ¾ teaspoon salt
2 tablespoons fresh lemon juice
Freshly ground black pepper

Put the oil in a wide pan and set over medium-high heat. When the oil is hot, put in the cinnamon, cardamom, and bay leaves. Stir for a few seconds. Put in the onion. Stir and fry until the onion pieces turn brown at the edges. Put in the garlic and stir for a few seconds. Put in the ginger and stir for another few seconds. Now put in the chicken (or turkey). Stir and fry until all the lumps are broken up. Now put in all the remaining ingredients. Stir to mix and cook for another 2 to 3 minutes, stirring as you do so.

Note: The whole spices—bay leaves, cinnamon stick, and cardamom pods—are not meant to be eaten.

SERVES 3–4

CHICKEN IN A CILANTRO, SPINACH, AND MUSTARD SAUCE

Hare masale vala murgh

■ ■ ■ ■ ■ ■ ■

I was trying to work out a quick version of a chicken dish seasoned with crushed mustard seeds and vinegar when it occurred to me that, instead of grinding the mustard seeds and soaking them in vinegar, I could just as easily use the grainy Pommery mustard that was sitting in a crock in my refrigerator. The taste would be almost the same and I would be saving a step! This particular mustard is labeled *Moutarde de Meaux*. It also says Pommery on the label. Any grainy French mustard will do.

You can serve this superb dish as part of a grand Indian meal or, as I sometimes do, with Indian Mashed Potatoes (page 90) and Simply Grilled Tomatoes (page 93). No other vegetable is needed as the sauce is almost entirely made up of spinach with the cilantro providing an extra dimension of flavor. Of course, you could always serve it with rice, plain boiled potatoes, or bread.

INGREDIENTS

¼ cup vegetable oil	Freshly ground black pepper
3 bay leaves	⅛ to ¼ teaspoon cayenne pepper
6 cardamom pods	2-inch piece fresh ginger, peeled and coarsely chopped
2-inch stick cinnamon	1 to 2 fresh, hot green chilies, sliced into coarse rings (do not remove seeds)
5 whole cloves	A generous fistful of fresh cilantro tops (Chinese parsley, fresh green coriander—use leaves and bits of tender stems)
2 dried, hot red chilies	
2¼ pounds chicken pieces, skinned and cut into serving portions (a pair of breasts into 4 to 6 pieces each, whole legs into 2 to 3 pieces each)	1 package (10 ounces) frozen, chopped spinach, boiled until it is just defrosted and then lightly drained
¼ cup golden raisins	3 tablespoons grainy mustard (Pommery Moutarde de Meaux; see recipe introduction)
6 tablespoons plain yogurt	
1¼ teaspoon salt	

Put the oil in a large, wide, nonstick pan (a large, nonstick frying pan is also quite suitable) and set over medium-high heat. When the oil is hot, put in the bay leaves, cardamom pods, cinnamon stick, cloves, and red chilies. Stir for a few seconds or until the bay leaves turn a few shades darker. Now put in the chicken pieces and brown well on both sides. Put in the raisins, stir for a few seconds, and put in the yogurt, 1 teaspoon salt, lots of freshly ground black pepper, and the cayenne. Stir and bring to a simmer. Cover tightly, turn the heat to low, and simmer gently for 15 minutes.

While the chicken simmers, put the ginger into the container of a blender along with 3 tablespoons water and blend until you have a smooth paste. Add the green chilies and cilantro and continue to blend, pushing down with a rubber spatula when necessary. Now put in the lightly drained spinach. Blend very briefly this time. The spinach should have a coarse texture and should not be a fine purée. Empty this green sauce into a bowl. Add the mustard and ¼ teaspoon salt. Mix.

When the chicken has cooked for 15 minutes, remove the cover and add the green sauce. Stir to mix. Bring to a simmer, cover again, and cook for about 10 minutes or until the chicken is tender. Turn the chicken pieces a few times during this period. Remove the bay leaves, cardamom pods, cinnamon stick, whole cloves, and dried chilies before serving.

SERVES 3–4

CHICKEN IN A SPICY RED SAUCE

Lal shorve vala murgh

∎ ∎ ∎ ∎ ∎ ∎

This dish of chicken and potatoes in a delicious red tomato sauce spiced up with cumin, cardamom, garlic, and ginger may be served with plain rice or with any Indian or Middle Eastern bread. I use canned chopped tomatoes but you could use whole canned ones. Just drain them briefly and then chop them very finely. Double the amount of fresh tomatoes, in season, may be used in the same way. You do not need to peel them.

I tend to use smallish chicken thighs but you can use any chicken part. A pair of breasts should be cut into 4 to 6 pieces each and whole legs into 2 to 3 pieces each. I skin all my chicken pieces but if you are in a great rush, you need not bother.

INGREDIENTS

2¼ pounds chicken pieces (see recipe introduction)	2-inch stick cinnamon
1 teaspoon salt or to taste	6 cardamom pods
Freshly ground black pepper	5 whole cloves
7 good-sized cloves garlic, peeled and coarsely chopped	3 dried, hot red chilies
2-inch piece fresh ginger, peeled and coarsely chopped	½ teaspoon ground turmeric
¼ cup vegetable oil	⅛ to ¼ teaspoon cayenne pepper
Generous pinch ground asafetida (page 132), optional	1½ cups canned, chopped tomatoes (see recipe introduction)
1 teaspoon cumin seeds	12 ounces potatoes, peeled and cut into 1½-inch chunks

Sprinkle the chicken pieces lightly with salt and black pepper and set aside.

Put the garlic and ginger into the container of a blender along with 3 tablespoons water and blend to a paste.

Put the oil in a wide, nonstick pan and set over medium-high heat. When the oil is hot, put in the *asafetida* if you are using it. A few seconds later, put in the cumin seeds. Wait for 10 seconds and put in the cinnamon stick, cardamom pods, cloves, and red chilies. Stir for a few seconds until the large spices begin to turn darker. Now put in the garlic and ginger. Stir and fry it for about 2 minutes. Put in the chicken, turmeric, and cayenne. Stir and fry for another minute. Now put in the chopped tomatoes, potatoes, 1¼ cups water, and 1 teaspoon salt. Bring to a boil. Cover, turn the heat to low and simmer gently for 25 to 30 minutes or until the chicken and potatoes are tender.

Note: This dish may be made a day ahead of time, kept covered in the refrigerator and then reheated. Remove the cinnamon stick, cardamom pods, whole cloves, and dried chilies before serving.

SERVES 3–4

ROYAL CHICKEN COOKED IN YOGURT

Shahi murgh

■■■■■■■

An elegant dish that may be served to the family or at a grand party. Rice is the ideal accompaniment.

INGREDIENTS

1 cup plain yogurt	3½ pounds chicken, cut into serving portions
1 teaspoon salt	¼ cup vegetable oil
Freshly ground black pepper	8 cardamom pods
1 teaspoon ground cumin	6 whole cloves
1 teaspoon ground coriander	2-inch stick cinnamon
¼ teaspoon cayenne pepper, or to taste	3 bay leaves
¼ cup finely chopped fresh cilantro (Chinese parsley, fresh green coriander)	2½ tablespoons blanched, slivered almonds
	2½ tablespoons golden raisins

Put the yogurt into a bowl. Beat it lightly until it is smooth and creamy. Add ½ teaspoon of the salt, some black pepper, the ground cumin, ground coriander, cayenne, and cilantro. Mix and set aside.

Using the remaining ½ teaspoon salt, season the chicken pieces on both sides and sprinkle on some freshly ground black pepper.

Put the oil in a wide, preferably nonstick pan and set over medium-high heat. When the oil is hot, put in the cardamom pods, cloves, cinnamon, and bay leaves. Stir once and put in some of the chicken pieces, only as many as the pan will hold easily in a single layer. Brown on both sides and remove to a large bowl. Brown all the chicken pieces this way and transfer them to the bowl. Put the almonds and raisins into the same hot oil. Stir quickly. The almonds should turn golden and the raisins should plump up—which will happen very fast. Now put the chicken and its accumulated juices back into the pan. Add the seasoned yogurt. Stir to mix and bring to a simmer. Cover, turn the heat to low, and simmer gently for 20 minutes, stirring once or twice during this time. Remove the cover, turn the heat up a bit, and reduce the sauce until it is thick and just clings to the chicken pieces. Turn the chicken pieces over gently as you do this.

Note: The large, whole spices—cardamom pods, whole cloves, cinnamon stick, and bay leaves—are not meant to be eaten.

SERVES 4

CHICKEN BREASTS BAKED WITH GREEN CHILIES AND ONIONS

Oven ki murghi

■ ■ ■ ■ ■ ■ ■

This gentle dish is elegant enough to be served at grand dinners. It can easily be doubled or tripled as the guest list expands and is equally perfect at a dinner for two. In fact, my husband and I dine on it frequently when we are by ourselves. The accompaniment of a simple rice dish and a vegetable or salad suffices for us. But if we are entertaining, I might serve Rice with Mushrooms and Mustard Seeds (page 102) and Cauliflower with Ginger, Garlic, and Green Chilies (page 83) as side dishes. This is a wonderful method for cooking chicken breasts. You will notice that they remain quite tender and very juicy.

INGREDIENTS

For the Sauce

2 tablespoons tomato paste

1 tablespoon Dijon mustard

1 teaspoon ground cumin

1 teaspoon store-bought garam masala *(page 134)*

1 tablespoon fresh lemon juice

½ teaspoon salt

⅛ to ¼ teaspoon cayenne pepper

1 cup heavy, whipping cream

You also need

4 boned, skinned chicken breast halves (about 1¼ pounds)

Salt as needed

Freshly ground black pepper

4 tablespoons vegetable oil

2-inch stick cinnamon

6 cardamom pods

6 whole cloves

1 medium-size onion (about 5 ounces), peeled and cut into fine half rings

1-inch piece fresh ginger, peeled and cut into fine slices, then into fine strips

1 to 3 fresh, hot green chilies, cut diagonally into fine strips (do not remove seeds)

½ teaspoon black or yellow mustard seeds

1 clove garlic, peeled and finely chopped

Preheat the oven to 350°F.

Put the tomato paste in a bowl; add 1 tablespoon water, and mix. Add all the remaining ingredients for the sauce in the order listed, mixing as you go.

Salt and pepper the chicken pieces generously on both sides.

Put 3 tablespoons of the oil in a nonstick frying pan and set over high heat. When the oil is hot, put in the cinnamon, cardamom pods, and cloves. Ten seconds later, put in the chicken pieces in a single layer and brown them lightly on both sides. Remove the chicken with a slotted spoon and place in an ovenproof dish in a single layer. Put the onion, ginger, and green chilies into the oil that remains in the frying pan. Stir and fry them until they are light brown in color. Remove with a slotted spoon and spread evenly over the chicken pieces.

Add the last tablespoon of oil to the frying pan and let it heat. Put in the mustard seeds. As soon as they pop—this takes just seconds—put in the garlic. Stir. As soon as it starts to brown, pour in the sauce. As soon as the sauce heats up and starts bubbling, pour it over and around the chicken without displacing the onion mixture. Place the ovenproof dish, uncovered, in the oven and bake for 25 minutes. Remove and discard the cinnamon stick, cardamom pods, and whole cloves and serve immediately.

SERVES 2–4

SPICY GRILLED CHICKEN

Masalewala murgh

∎ ∎ ∎ ∎ ∎ ∎ ∎

Sometimes, after a long day at work, the easiest dish to put at the table is grilled chicken. Most Indian versions require a marinating period, but if you are rushed, as I am most of the time, follow this recipe and you will come up with delicious results—fast.

You may be surprised at my use of oregano but it tastes a bit like our Indian *ajwain* and is much easier to find.

This chicken may be served Western-style with boiled potatoes and a green vegetable or salad. You may also serve it with rice and an Indian vegetable, such as Green Peas in a Creamy Sauce (page 87).

The spice paste may be prepared up to a day ahead of time, covered, and refrigerated. You can also rub the chicken pieces with the spice paste and refrigerate them, covered, for up to 24 hours before grilling.

INGREDIENTS

For the Spice Paste	*1¼ teaspoons salt*
1 tablespoon coarsely crushed black peppercorns	*1 clove garlic, peeled and crushed*
1 tablespoon paprika (bright red, if possible)	*3 tablespoons vegetable oil*
½ teaspoon cayenne pepper or to taste	*2 tablespoons fresh lemon juice*
1 tablespoon store bought garam masala *(page 134)*	*2 tablespoons plain yogurt*
2 teaspoons ground cumin	
2 teaspoons dried oregano or 1 teaspoon ajwain *seeds (see recipe introduction)*	***You also need***
	2¾ pounds chicken pieces

Preheat the grill and arrange the grilling rack at least 5 to 6 inches from the heat source. If you can control your heat, set it at medium-high.

Combine all the ingredients for the spice paste in a bowl and mix well. Rub the paste over the chicken as evenly as possible. Arrange the chicken pieces on the grill in a single layer, with the fleshier parts up and the skin side down. Grill for 10 to 12 minutes or until browned. You may need to rearrange some of the pieces so that they all brown evenly. Turn the pieces over and cook the second side the same way.

SERVES 4

CHICKEN, RED LENTILS, AND GREEN BEANS IN ONE POT

Ek handi ka murgh aur masoor

■ ■ ■ ■ ■ ■ ■

Even though this dish takes 45 minutes to make from start to finish, almost everything you need for the meal, except the rice or bread, is in the one pan—poultry, lentils, green vegetable, even tomatoes. If you leave out the chilies, this is a perfect dish for children.

There are, indeed, quite a lot of ingredients to this recipe. Do not let that put you off. This *is* an easy dish to prepare and delicious besides.

INGREDIENTS

6 tablespoons vegetable oil	Freshly ground black pepper
3 bay leaves	1½ teaspoons store-bought garam masala (page 134)
5 whole cloves	1½ tablespoons fresh lemon juice
6 cardamom pods	6 ounces green beans, trimmed and cut into 1-inch lengths
2-inch stick cinnamon	Generous pinch asafetida (page 132), optional
3 dried hot red chilies	1½ teaspoons cumin seeds
2 pounds chicken pieces, skinned and cut into smaller serving portions (a pair of breasts into 4 to 6 pieces each and whole legs into 2 to 3 pieces each)	1 small onion (about 4 ounces), peeled and cut into fine half rings
1⅔ cups red lentils (masoor dal), picked over, washed, and drained	2 cloves garlic, peeled and finely chopped
	1 teaspoon ground cumin
	1 teaspoon ground coriander
½ teaspoon ground turmeric	⅛ to ¼ teaspoon cayenne pepper (optional)
2 teaspoons salt	12 cherry tomatoes, cut into halves crosswise, or 1 medium-sized tomato (about 5 ounces), diced

Put 3 tablespoons of the oil into a wide, nonstick pan and set over high heat. When the oil is hot, put in the bay leaves, cloves, cardamom pods, cinnamon stick, and red chilies. Stir once or twice until the bay leaf starts to darken. Quickly put in the chicken pieces in a single layer and brown on both sides. Remove and spread out on a plate, leaving the oil and spices behind. Take the pan off the heat briefly and put into it the lentils, turmeric, and 5 cups water. Put it back on high heat and bring to a simmer. Cover partially and cook gently for 20 minutes.

Meanwhile, sprinkle ½ teaspoon of the salt, lots of black pepper, ½ teaspoon of the *garam masala,* and the lemon juice on both sides of the chicken pieces. Rub in and set aside. When the lentils have cooked for 20 minutes, put in the chicken and all its accumulated juices, the green beans, and 1½ teaspoons salt. Stir and bring to a simmer. Cover, turn the heat to low, and cook gently for another 20 minutes, stirring now and then.

Two minutes before the chicken and lentils are cooked, put the remaining 3 tablespoons oil in a medium-sized frying pan and set over high heat. When the oil is hot, put in the *asafetida* (if you are using it) and, a second later, the cumin seeds. Ten seconds later, put in the onion. Stir and fry until the onion turns brown at the edges. Put in the garlic. Stir and fry until the onion has turned fairly brown. Add the ground cumin, ground coriander, 1 teaspoon *garam masala,* and the cayenne if you want the dish to be hot. Stir once. Now put in the tomatoes, stir for 20 seconds, and pour this entire mixture into the pan with the chicken and lentils. Stir to mix.

SERVES 4–6

FISH AND SEAFOOD

▪▪▪▪▪▪▪

There is nothing quite as good as fresh fish, and more and more seems to be finding its way into our markets these days. For this I am very thankful. Fresh fish fillets and steaks can be quickly fried or grilled with lavish sprinklings of mouthwatering spices. But we should not discount some canned and frozen fish. You will find here a superb recipe for canned tuna, filled with slivers of fresh ginger, green chilies, and cilantro. Squid and shrimp freeze very well when they are flash-frozen at sea. Both cook in minutes and can be combined with green sauces, coconut sauces, or spicy tomato-based sauces—whatever your fancy desires.

▪▪▪▪▪▪▪

■■■■■■■

■■■■■■■

CURRIED TUNA

Tuna ki kari

■ ■ ■ ■ ■ ■

This recipe, which is as good as it is simple, comes from Chun Kern, my friend from the Himalayan hills who now lives in the United States. You may eat this tuna in sandwiches, on toast, take it on picnics (I always do), or use it as a stuffing for "turnover"-type patties made with store-bought puff pastry. It is also excellent eaten plain with a variety of salads.

Use a good-quality canned tuna packed in oil. I do not drain it as the oil prevents the tuna from drying out. Also, a good curry powder provides a useful short cut. I happen to like Bolst's hot curry powder (available at gourmet specialty shops), but use whichever one you like.

INGREDIENTS

1½ tablespoons vegetable oil

1 small onion (2 ounces), peeled and cut into very fine half rings

1 clove garlic, peeled and very finely chopped

1 teaspoon curry powder

1 can (6 ounces) good-quality tuna, packed in oil

½ to 1 fresh, hot green chili, cut into very fine rounds (do not remove seeds)

½-inch piece fresh ginger, peeled and cut into very fine slices, then into very fine strips

2 to 3 tablespoons chopped fresh cilantro (Chinese parsley, fresh green coriander)

Salt to taste

Freshly ground black pepper

Put the oil in a nonstick frying pan and set over medium-high heat. When the oil is hot, put in the onion and garlic. Stir and fry until the onion turns brown at the edges. Put in the curry powder. Stir once or twice. Put in the tuna. Stir it around and break up any big lumps. Turn the heat to low. Add the green chili, ginger, and cilantro. Stir to mix. Check for salt, adding if needed. Add a generous amount of black pepper. Mix well and remove from the heat. Serve hot, at room temperature, or cold.

SERVES 2–3

SHRIMP STEAMED WITH MUSTARD SEEDS

Chingri bhapey

■ ■ ■ ■ ■ ■

Very few people in the West associate the technique of gentle steaming with Indian cuisine. And yet, in many regions of India, such as the east and the south, steaming is common, and steaming utensils are standard equipment in every kitchen.

This simple yet stunning dish is a Bengali classic. Fish—in Bengal it would be pieces of *hilsa,* a kind of freshwater mackerel, or shrimp—are put into a paste of crushed mustard seeds and mustard oil and left to steam briefly until the fish just turns opaque. The results are spectacular. The fish turns silken and the sauce created by the steam and the sweating fish is magically sweet and pungent. The dish is always eaten with plain rice.

Mustard oil is sold by Indian grocers. It is a good oil to know about. Pungent when raw, it turns comfortingly sweet when heated. Good-quality fish is essential here. Pieces of fresh haddock can be substituted for the prawns if you so desire.

You may use one of two methods for steaming:

Put the bowl of shrimp into a large saucepan. Pour boiling water into the pan so that it comes one-third of the way up the sides of the bowl. Cover the saucepan and steam.

Put water in the bottom third of a large wok. Bring to a boil. Put a bamboo steaming tray or a perforated metal steaming tray on top of the water. Place the bowl of shrimp on the tray, cover the wok, and steam.

INGREDIENTS

1½ teaspoons black mustard seeds	¼ teaspoon cayenne pepper
1 tablespoon finely chopped onion	3 tablespoons mustard oil
1 fresh, hot green chili, finely chopped (do not remove seeds)	1 pound medium-sized shrimp, peeled, deveined, and washed
¼ teaspoon ground turmeric	(page 131), then drained
⅓ teaspoon salt	

Grind the mustard seeds coarsely in the container of a clean coffee grinder or other spice grinder. Put into a medium-sized stainless steel, ceramic, or ovenproof glass bowl. Add 1 tablespoon water and mix. Add the onion, green chili, turmeric, salt, cayenne, and mustard oil. Mix again. Now put in the shrimp and mix. Cover with a piece of aluminum foil and set aside for 10 minutes as you get your steaming equipment ready. Steam, covered, for about 10 minutes or until the shrimp just turn opaque all the way through. Stir the shrimp once after about 6 minutes, remembering to cover the bowl and the steaming utensil again.

SERVES 4

GRILLED FISH STEAKS

Grill macchi

■ ■ ■ ■ ■ ■

Fish steaks usually come with a central bone, but chunky pieces of filleted haddock, salmon, and fresh tuna may also be cooked as steaks. With the bone, 1½ pounds of fish steaks might serve just two people. Without the bone, they would serve four. You can use anything from cod, halibut, and haddock to fresh tuna, swordfish, and salmon.

INGREDIENTS

1½ pounds fish steaks or thick pieces of filleted fish (see recipe introduction)	*1 teaspoon store-bought* garam masala *(page 134)*
Salt to taste	*3 tablespoons melted butter or vegetable oil*
2 teaspoons freshly ground black pepper	*1 tablespoon grainy mustard (Pommery* Moutarde de Meaux, *see page 135)*
½ teaspoon ground turmeric	*½ cup heavy, whipping cream*
¼ teaspoon cayenne pepper	*Lemon wedges*

Spread out the fish steaks in a single layer. Sprinkle adequately on both sides with salt and then with the black pepper, turmeric, cayenne, and *garam masala*. Pat the spices in and set aside for 15 minutes.

Preheat the grill.

Dribble half the melted butter or oil over one side of the fish pieces and grill them about 4 inches from the heat source for 2 to 3 minutes or until they are just starting to brown. Mix the mustard and cream and brush the fish with half of the mixture. Grill for another 2 minutes or so until the fish is golden brown. Turn the pieces over and repeat the process, first with a brushing of butter or oil and then with the remaining mustard and cream mixture. Serve hot with the lemon wedges.

SERVES 2–4

FRIED FISH STEAKS

Tali macchi

∎∎∎∎∎∎

Cod steaks with bone are ideal for this very satisfying dish although any fish steaks may be used. They may be served as part of an Indian meal or Western-style with boiled potatoes and a salad or cooked vegetable.

INGREDIENTS

3 medium-sized cod steaks (about 7 to 8 ounces each)
⅓ to ½ teaspoon salt
½ to ¾ teaspoon freshly ground black pepper
¼ teaspoon ground turmeric
¼ teaspoon cayenne pepper or to taste

½ teaspoon store-bought garam masala *(page 134)*
1 tablespoon all-purpose flour
¼ cup vegetable oil
3 lemon wedges

Lay the fish pieces out in a single layer on a big plate. Dust evenly on both sides with the salt, black pepper, turmeric, cayenne, and *garam masala*. Rub in the spices. Now dust both sides with the flour and let the steaks sit for 10 to 15 minutes.

Put the oil in a large frying pan and set over medium-high heat. When the oil is hot, put in the steaks in a single layer. When one side turns golden brown, turn over the fish pieces carefully and brown the second side as well. The fish is done when it is just cooked through. Remove with a slotted spatula and serve with the lemon wedges.

SERVES 3

FISH IN A GREEN SAUCE

Haray masale ki macchi

■ ■ ■ ■ ■ ■ ■

You need steaks from a firm-fleshed fish here. Kingfish and salmon are ideal but cod would do as well. I season the fish first and let it marinate while I prepare the ingredients for the green sauce.

INGREDIENTS

For Marinating the Fish

2 good-sized steaks (about ¾ pound each) from a salmon or kingfish (see recipe introduction)

Salt to taste

Freshly ground black pepper

⅛ teaspoon ground turmeric

⅛ teaspoon cayenne pepper

For the Green Sauce

3 tablespoons vegetable oil

⅓ cup (3 ounces) peeled and finely chopped onion

2 cloves garlic, peeled and finely chopped

1 cup finely chopped fresh cilantro (Chinese parsley, fresh green coriander)

1 medium-sized tomato, finely chopped

2 to 3 fresh, hot green chilies (do not remove seeds)

1 teaspoon peeled, finely grated fresh ginger

1 tablespoon fresh lemon juice

⅛ teaspoon salt or to taste

⅛ teaspoon cayenne pepper

½ teaspoon store-bought garam masala *(page 134)*

Rub the fish well on both sides with a generous sprinkling of salt, lots of freshly ground pepper, and the turmeric, and cayenne pepper and set aside.

Put the oil in a nonstick frying pan and set over high heat. When the oil is hot, put in the fish and brown quickly on both sides without letting it cook through. Remove with a slotted spoon and set aside. Put in the onion and garlic. Stir and fry until the onion browns a bit. Put in the cilantro, tomato, green chilies, ginger, lemon juice, and salt. Stir and cook over medium-high heat until the cilantro and tomato have completely wilted. Spread the green sauce around in the frying pan and check the salt. Lay the fish over the top. Now spoon some green sauce over the fish. Sprinkle the cayenne and *garam masala* over the top. Bring to a simmer. Cover, lower the heat, and simmer gently for about 10 minutes.

SERVES 2

STIR-FRIED SHRIMP IN AN AROMATIC TOMATO-CREAM SAUCE

Bhagari jhinga

■ ■ ■ ■ ■ ■

One of the aromas that I find very refreshing in this particular dish is that of fresh curry leaves. I know that they are not always easy to find. Whenever you do come across them, get an extra supply and freeze them immediately in flat plastic bags. They hold up quite well. If you can get only dried curry leaves, mix them into the cream sauce instead of frying them with the shrimp. If you cannot get them at all, just do without. The dish will still taste superb. To take fresh curry leaves off the stem, just pull along the stem with your thumb and first finger and they will come right off!

The sauce can be made several hours ahead of time and refrigerated. The shrimp could be peeled, deveined, washed, patted dry, and left covered in the refrigerator overnight, if necessary. The actual cooking takes just a few minutes. This dish is best served with rice.

INGREDIENTS

For the Sauce
1 tablespoon tomato paste
¾ teaspoon salt
¼ teaspoon sugar
1 teaspoon store-bought garam masala *(page 134)*
½ teaspoon ground roasted cumin seeds *(page 133)*
⅛ to ¼ teaspoon cayenne pepper or to taste
3 tablespoons finely chopped cilantro *(Chinese parsley, fresh green coriander)*
1 fresh, hot green chili, finely chopped *(do not remove seeds)*
1 tablespoon fresh lemon juice

1 small can *(7 ounces)* coconut milk, well stirred, or ⅞ cup heavy, whipping cream

For Stir-Frying the Shrimp
3 tablespoons vegetable oil
1 teaspoon black mustard seeds
3 cloves garlic, peeled and finely chopped
10 to 15 fresh curry leaves *(recipe introduction and page 134)*, optional
1¼ pounds medium-sized shrimp, peeled, deveined, and washed *(page 131)*, then patted dry

To make the sauce: Put the tomato paste in a bowl. Add the salt, sugar, *garam masala*, ground roasted cumin seeds, cayenne, cilantro, green chili, lemon juice, dried curry leaves, if you are not using fresh leaves with the shrimp, and 1 tablespoon water. Mix well. Slowly add the coconut milk or cream, mixing as you go. Set aside.

To stir-fry the shrimp: Put the oil in a wok or frying pan and set over medium-high heat. When the oil is hot, put in the mustard seeds. As soon as the mustard seeds begin to pop—this takes just a few seconds—put in the garlic and fresh curry leaves, if using. Stir until the garlic turns medium brown and put in the shrimp. Stir until the shrimp turn opaque most of the way through. Add the sauce, turn the heat to medium, and heat the sauce through until it begins to simmer. By then the shrimp should be completely opaque and cooked through. Turn off the heat.

SERVES 4–5

SQUID OR SCALLOPS IN SPINACH-TOMATO CURRY SAUCE

Samundar ki kari

■ ■ ■ ■ ■ ■

If you are rushed, it is best to buy cleaned squid. Frozen squid usually comes all cleaned and is totally acceptable. Directions for cleaning fresh squid are on page 131. Once cleaned, the squid's tubular body should be cut into ¼-inch-wide rings. The head area and tentacles may be left whole or halved. Scallops, of course, are sold ready for cooking. You could, if you like, make it with peeled shrimp.

This dish may be eaten with rice or, oddly enough, with noodles. It is superb for entertaining.

INGREDIENTS

½ teaspoon cayenne pepper

½ teaspoon ground turmeric

1 teaspoon ground cumin

1 teaspoon ground coriander

1⅛ teaspoons salt

Freshly ground black pepper

1 teaspoon grainy mustard (Pommery Moutarde de Meaux, see page 135)

3 tablespoons vegetable oil

1 teaspoon black or yellow mustard seeds

3 to 4 cloves garlic, peeled and finely chopped

½-inch piece fresh ginger, peeled and finely chopped

¾ cup canned chopped tomatoes or lightly drained, canned whole tomatoes, finely chopped

4 ounces fresh spinach, cut, crosswise, into fine strips

1¼ pounds cleaned, sliced squid (see recipe introduction) or whole scallops

½ cup canned coconut milk, well stirred, or heavy, whipping cream

Combine the cayenne, turmeric, cumin, coriander, salt, black pepper, mustard, and 2 tablespoons water in a small bowl. Mix well. Put the oil in a large, nonstick frying pan and set over high heat. When the oil is hot, put in the whole mustard seeds. As soon as they begin to pop—a matter of seconds—put in the garlic and ginger. Stir and fry until the garlic turns a light brown. Add the spice paste. Stir and fry for 15 seconds. Put in the tomatoes and spinach. Stir and cook for a minute. Add 1 cup water and bring to a simmer. Simmer, uncovered, on low heat for 10 minutes. Put in the squid or scallops. Turn the heat to high. Stir and cook until the squid or scallops just turn opaque. This will happen quite fast. Put in the coconut milk or cream and bring to a simmer. Stir and simmer for half a minute. Turn off the heat and serve.

SERVES 4

SPICY GRILLED FISH

Masaledar macchi

∎∎∎∎∎∎

Fish is grilled all along India's coastline, and various marinades and basting sauces are used. Sometimes the grilling is done over rice straw, at other times over smoldering coconut husks. In the north, fish is often grilled—quick-baked might be a better description—in a *tandoor*. I have used my indoor grill here but you could also grill outdoors over charcoal.

What helps the grilling enormously is a hinged, double-racked holder. The fish is placed securely inside it. It can then be turned and basted with ease. Such racks are sold by shops specializing in kitchen equipment. If you cannot find one, just oil your grill rack well and lay your fish directly on it.

INGREDIENTS

1¼ pounds fish such as a trout, salmon trout, or small salmon, scaled and cleaned but left whole
½ teaspoon salt
3 tablespoons fresh lemon juice
¼ cup (2 ounces) peeled and coarsely chopped onion
2 cloves garlic, peeled and coarsely chopped
1-inch piece fresh ginger

1 fresh, hot green chili, sliced (do not remove seeds)
¼ teaspoon ground turmeric
1 teaspoon store-bought garam masala *(page 134)*
¼ teaspoon cayenne pepper
¾ cup canned coconut milk, well stirred
Vegetable oil for grilling

Wash the fish well and pat dry. Cut 3 or 4 deep, diagonal slits across both sides of the fish. Rub with ½ teaspoon salt and 1 tablespoon of the lemon juice. Set aside as you make the marinade.

Combine the remaining 2 tablespoons lemon juice, ¼ teaspoon salt, onion, garlic, ginger, green chili, turmeric, *garam masala,* and cayenne in the container of an electric blender and blend until smooth. Empty the paste into a shallow dish large enough to hold the fish. Add the coconut milk and mix. Now put the fish into the dish and rub with the marinade. Leave for 5 to 10 minutes.

Meanwhile, preheat the grill and oil the grilling rack with a little vegetable oil. The rack should be placed about 6 inches from the heat source.

Lift the fish out of the marinade and place it in (or on) the rack. Grill for about 25 minutes, turning the fish every 5 minutes and basting frequently with the marinade. If you do not have a hinged rack, turn only once, midway through the cooking, using the flat side of a large chef's knife. If the fish is browning too fast, distance it from the source of heat. To allow a crust to form over the fish, do not baste toward the end.

SERVES 2–3

FISH FILLETS IN A CURRY SAUCE

"Curry" dar macchi

■ ■ ■ ■ ■ ■

Bland white sauces were anathema to the Indian cooks who presided over Anglo-Indian households so they invariably added a few local seasonings in order to perk them up. Here is one such dish.

You may use any fish fillets—cod, haddock, and halibut—although fillets of dark, oily fish, such as bluefish and mackerel, are ideal. Get thick fillets if possible and, if the skin can be removed, so much the better.

INGREDIENTS

2 pounds thick fish fillet or fillets (see recipe introduction)

2¼ cups milk

1 teaspoon salt

Lots of freshly ground black pepper

½ teaspoon cayenne pepper

¼ teaspoon ground turmeric

5 tablespoons bread crumbs (made from dried bread—homemade or store-bought)

4 tablespoons butter (½ stick) unsalted butter

¼ cup good curry powder

2 tablespoons all-purpose flour

3 tablespoons finely chopped fresh cilantro (Chinese parsley, fresh green coriander)

2 to 3 teaspoons fresh lemon juice

Arrange a shelf in the upper third of the oven and preheat the oven to its highest temperature.

Spread out the fish in a baking dish. Combine the milk, salt, pepper, cayenne, and turmeric in a pitcher and pour over the fish. Set aside for 15 minutes. (Use this time to get all the remaining ingredients measured and chopped.) Then lift the fish out of the milk and dust both sides with the bread crumbs, patting them on so that they adhere. Reserve the milk. Now put the fish in a shallow baking dish lined with aluminum foil. Dot with 2 tablespoons of the butter and bake for 15 minutes.

While the fish bakes, set the milk to heat but do not boil. Melt the remaining 2 tablespoons butter in a small, heavy saucepan over medium-low heat. When it has melted and is bubbling, put in the curry powder. Stir for a minute. Now put in the flour. Stir for about 2 minutes. It should keep bubbling.

Take the saucepan off the heat and, using a whisk, beat in the hot milk. Now put the saucepan on medium-high heat and stir with the whisk until the sauce comes to a boil. Boil for a minute, whisking all the time. Add the cilantro and lemon juice. Stir to mix them in.

Put the fish on a serving plate or on individual plates. Pour the sauce over the top and serve immediately. Extra sauce, if there is any, may be served on the side.

SERVES 4–5

LEGUMES AND VEGETABLES

■■■■■■■

Legumes and vegetables are the heart of traditional Indian meals. Most legumes cook slowly—and for a long time. I have included only those that can be prepared quickly, such as red lentils and whole green lentils and even canned chickpeas (garbanzo beans) that just need dressing up. As for the vegetables, nearly all of them cook quickly. I have chosen recipes that are quite simple to put together.

■■■■■■■

■■■■■■

■■■■■■

MUSHROOM CURRY

Shorvedar khumbi

∎∎∎∎∎∎∎

I have used ordinary white mushrooms here but you may make this with almost any seasonal mushrooms. Whichever kind you get, cut them into large, chunky pieces so they do not get lost in the sauce.

INGREDIENTS

1½-inch piece fresh ginger, peeled and chopped	1 teaspoon tomato paste
1 small onion (about 4 ounces), peeled and chopped	2 teaspoons ground coriander
3 cloves garlic, peeled and chopped	¾ teaspoon salt
1 pound large fresh mushrooms	⅛ to ¼ teaspoon cayenne pepper
6 tablespoons vegetable oil	2 tablespoons chopped fresh cilantro (Chinese parsley, fresh
3 tablespoons plain yogurt	green coriander)

Put the ginger, onion, and garlic into the container of an electric blender along with 3 tablespoons water and blend until smooth.

Wipe the mushrooms with a damp cloth and cut them into halves or quarters, depending upon size.

Put 3 tablespoons of the oil in a nonstick frying pan and set over high heat. When the oil is hot, put in the mushrooms. Stir and fry for 2 to 3 minutes or until the mushrooms have lost their raw look. Empty the contents of the pan into a bowl. Wipe the pan.

Put the remaining 3 tablespoons oil into the pan and set over high heat. When the oil is hot, put in the paste from the blender. Stir and fry for 3 to 4 minutes until it starts turning brown. Add 1 tablespoon of the yogurt and fry for 30 seconds. Add another tablespoon of the yogurt and fry for 30 seconds. Do this a third time. Now put in the tomato paste and fry for 30 seconds. Put in the ground coriander and stir once or twice. Now put in 1¼ cups water, the mushrooms and their juices, salt, and cayenne pepper. Stir and bring to a simmer. Turn the heat to low and simmer for 5 minutes. Sprinkle the cilantro over the top before serving.

SERVES 4

RED LENTILS TARKA

Masoor dal

■ ■ ■ ■ ■ ■

Indians tend to eat protein-rich legumes with many everyday meals. Often these are prepared with just a flavoring, or *tarka*, of whole cumin seeds, *asafetida* and whole chilies popped in hot oil or *ghee*. Mustard seeds and a choice of garlic, curry leaves, onions, even tomatoes may be added to this *tarka*. I have used red lentils here, partly because they are sold by all health food shops and make the shopping very easy, but mainly because they cook faster than most other traditional *dals* (split peas). Serve this dish with plain rice and a simple meat or vegetable. Yogurt relishes and pickles make good accompaniments.

INGREDIENTS

1½ cups red lentils (masoor dal)	*Generous pinch of ground* asafetida *(page 132)*
½ teaspoon ground turmeric	*1 teaspoon cumin seeds*
1¼ to 1½ teaspoons salt	*3 to 5 dried, hot red chilies*
3 tablespoons vegetable oil or ghee *(page 135)*	

Pick over the lentils and wash in several changes of water. Drain. Put in a heavy saucepan. Add 5 cups water and the turmeric. Stir and bring to a simmer. (Do not let it boil over.) Cover in such a way as to leave the lid just very slightly ajar, turn the heat to low, and simmer gently for 35 to 40 minutes or until tender. Stir a few times during the cooking. Add the salt and mix. Leave covered, on very low heat, as you do the next step.

Put the oil in a small frying pan and set over medium-high heat. When the oil is hot, put in the *asafetida;* then, a second later, the cumin seeds. Let the cumin seeds sizzle for a few seconds. Put in the red chilies. As soon as they turn dark red (this takes just a few seconds), lift up the lid of the lentil pan and pour in the contents of the frying pan, oil as well as spices. Cover the saucepan immediately to trap the aromas.

SERVES 6–8

WHOLE GREEN LENTILS WITH CILANTRO AND MINT

Sabut peeli massoor

■ ■ ■ ■ ■ ■

For speed, I use a pressure cooker although you could cook the lentils in any ordinary saucepan for 50 to 60 minutes. You would need to increase the water by 1¼ cups. If you cannot get fresh mint, use more cilantro.

INGREDIENTS

3 tablespoons vegetable oil

½ teaspoon cumin seeds

½ teaspoon black or yellow mustard seeds

Pinch of ground asafetida (page 132), optional

1 to 3 dried, hot red chilies

1 small onion (4 ounces), peeled and cut into fine half rings

2 cloves garlic, peeled and chopped

1 medium-sized tomato, chopped

1 cup whole green lentils

¾ teaspoon salt

1 teaspoon ground coriander

½ cup chopped fresh cilantro (Chinese parsley, fresh green coriander)

½ cup chopped fresh mint

Put the oil in a pressure cooker and set over medium-high heat. When the oil is hot, put in the cumin and mustard seeds. As soon as the mustard seeds begin to pop—this takes just a few seconds—put in the *asafetida* and the red chilies. Stir once. Put in the onion, garlic, and tomato. Stir for about 2 minutes or until the onion browns a bit. Now put in the lentils, 3½ cups water, salt, ground coriander, cilantro, and mint. Stir and bring to a simmer. Cover, turn the heat to high, and bring up to pressure. Turn the heat down to low and cook at full pressure for 15 minutes. Take off the heat and reduce the pressure with cool water.

Stir and serve.

SERVES 4

CAULIFLOWER WITH GINGER, GARLIC, AND GREEN CHILIES

Sookhi gobi

■ ■ ■ ■ ■ ■

A simple, everyday dish. The special taste comes from allowing the florets to brown slightly. Do not cut them too small or they might fall apart.

INGREDIENTS

3 tablespoons vegetable oil

½ teaspoon cumin seeds

½ teaspoon yellow mustard seeds

3 cloves garlic, peeled and finely chopped

1-inch piece fresh ginger, peeled and cut into fine shreds

1 pound (4 heaping cups) cauliflower florets

1 to 3 fresh, hot green chilies

¾ teaspoon salt

Freshly ground black pepper

½ teaspoon store-bought garam masala *(page 134)*

⅛ teaspoon cayenne pepper or to taste

Put the oil in a wok and set over medium-high heat. When the oil is hot, put in the cumin and mustard seeds. As soon as the mustard seeds begin to pop—this just takes a few seconds—put in the garlic, ginger, cauliflower, and green chilies, all at the same time. Stir and fry for 5 to 7 minutes or until the cauliflower has turned somewhat brown. Now put in the salt, black pepper, *garam masala*, and cayenne and give the florets a good toss. Put in ¼ cup water and cover the wok immediately. Cook for 2 minutes and serve.

SERVES 3–4

GENTLY STEWED BEETS

Taridar chukandar

∎∎∎∎∎∎∎

Any beets may be used for this stewlike dish. My own favorite happens to be Chioggia, a very ancient Italian variety. These beets are small and sweet, with radish-red skin and striated red-and-pale-yellow flesh. I do not mean to sound like a garden catalog, but these are certainly worth knowing about, if not growing. Mine are supplied by a local farmer.

INGREDIENTS

2 pounds beets without stems and leaves

3 tablespoons vegetable oil

1 teaspoon cumin seeds

1 bay leaf

1 cup canned chopped tomatoes or lightly drained, canned whole tomatoes, chopped

1 teaspoon ground cumin

1 teaspoon ground coriander

¼ teaspoon ground turmeric

¼ teaspoon cayenne pepper

¾ teaspoon salt

Peel the beets and cut them into 1-inch chunks.

Put the oil in a wide, medium-sized pan and set over high heat. When the oil is hot, put in the cumin seeds and bay leaf. As soon as the bay leaf darkens slightly—this takes just seconds—put in the tomatoes, ground cumin, ground coriander, turmeric, cayenne, beets, salt, and 1½ cups water. Stir and bring to a boil. Cover, turn the heat to low and simmer for 30 to 40 minutes or until the beets are tender.

SERVES 4–6

GREEN BEANS WITH MUSHROOMS

Sem aur khumbi

■ ■ ■ ■ ■ ■ ■

A hearty dish that may be served as part of a vegetarian meal or with any meat, poultry, or fish.

INGREDIENTS

5 tablespoons vegetable oil	*2 teaspoons ground coriander*
¾ teaspoon cumin seeds	*1½ teaspoons ground cumin*
2 small onions (8 ounces in all), peeled and cut into fine half rings	*½ teaspoon ground turmeric*
1-inch piece fresh ginger, peeled and cut into slivers	*¾ teaspoon store-bought* garam masala *(page 134)*
5 cloves garlic, peeled and chopped	*¾ teaspoon cayenne pepper*
8 ounces fresh mushrooms, sliced thickly	*1 teaspoon salt*
1 pound green beans, trimmed and cut into 2-inch segments	*1 medium-sized tomato, coarsely chopped*

Put the oil in a wide pan and set over medium-high heat. When the oil is hot, put in the cumin seeds. As soon as the seeds begin to sizzle, put in the onion. Stir and fry until the onion browns. Put in the ginger and garlic. Stir until the garlic starts to brown. Put in the mushrooms. Stir and fry for 2 minutes. Put in the beans, ground coriander, ground cumin, turmeric, *garam masala,* cayenne, salt, tomato, and ½ cup water. Bring to a boil. Cover, lower the heat and simmer for 15 minutes. Remove the cover, raise the heat, and boil most of the liquid away, stirring gently as you do so.

SERVES 4

GREEN PEAS IN A CREAMY SAUCE

Matar makhani

■ ■ ■ ■ ■ ■ ■

This is a recipe in which frozen peas can be used to great advantage. The sauce takes just minutes to put together and may be made up to a day in advance and refrigerated, if you so prefer. This dish may be served with all Indian meals. It also goes well with lamb and pork roasts.

INGREDIENTS

¼ teaspoon sugar

½ teaspoon ground cumin

½ teaspoon homemade garam masala (page 134)

¾ teaspoon salt

¼ to ½ teaspoon cayenne pepper

1 tablespoon tomato paste

¾ cup heavy, whipping cream

1 tablespoon fresh lemon juice

2 tablespoons chopped fresh cilantro (Chinese parsley, fresh green coriander)

1 fresh, hot green chili, finely chopped (do not remove seeds)

3 tablespoons vegetable oil

½ teaspoon cumin seeds

½ teaspoon black or yellow mustard seeds

2 packages packets frozen peas (10 ounces each), completely defrosted under warm water and drained

Combine the sugar, ground cumin, *garam masala,* salt, cayenne, and tomato paste. Slowly add 2 tablespoons water, mixing as you go. Add the cream slowly and mix. Put in the lemon juice, cilantro, and green chili. Mix again and set this cream sauce aside.

Put the oil in a large frying pan and set over medium-high heat. When the oil is hot, put in the cumin seeds and mustard seeds. As soon as the mustard seeds begin to pop—this takes just a few seconds—put in the peas. Stir and fry the peas for 30 seconds. Put in the cream sauce. Cook on high heat for about 1½ to 2 minutes or until the sauce has thickened, stirring gently as you do so.

SERVES 5–6

STIR-FRIED GREEN CABBAGE WITH FENNEL SEEDS

Bhuni bandh gobi

■■■■■■

The cabbage and onions get nicely browned here and taste gloriously of fennel. You could easily serve this with Western-style sausages, ham, pork chops, or any kind of roast pork meat, or with roast lamb or even duck or venison.

INGREDIENTS

1½ pounds green cabbage (half a large head)
¼ cup vegetable oil
¾ teaspoon cumin seeds
½ teaspoon fennel seeds
1 teaspoon sesame seeds
1 medium-large onion (7 ounces), peeled and cut, lengthwise, into fine half rings

1 teaspoon salt
⅛ to ¼ teaspoon cayenne pepper
1 tablespoon fresh lemon juice
½ teaspoon store-bought garam masala *(page 134)*

Remove the coarse outer leaves of the cabbage. If you have a cabbage half, cut it in half again, lengthwise, and then core the sections. Now cut each section, lengthwise, into very fine, long shreds. A bread knife is ideal for this. (You could also use a food processor.)

Put the oil in a wide, preferably nonstick pan, and set over medium-high heat. When the oil is hot, put in the cumin, fennel, and sesame seeds. As soon as the sesame seeds begin to pop, put in the onion. Stir and fry for 3 to 4 minutes or until the onion has browned a bit. Put in the cabbage. Stir and fry for about 6 minutes or until the cabbage too has browned somewhat. Now put in the salt and cayenne. Turn down the heat to medium-low and cook, stirring now and then, for another 7 to 8 minutes or until the onions appear caramelized and soft. Add the lemon juice and *garam masala*. Stir to mix.

SERVES 4

INDIAN MASHED POTATOES

Mash aloo

■■■■■■

Indians are always using spicy mashed potatoes to make potato patties and deep-fried potato balls, so it occurred to me that the same mixture could be served plain—and that it would be wonderful with all manner of fish, poultry and meat dishes. I tried it out, and it *was* wonderful. Here it is.

INGREDIENTS

2¼ pounds potatoes, peeled and cut into large chunks
¾ cup milk, heated, plus more if needed
4 to 6 tablespoons butter (½ to ¾ stick), cut into pieces
1¼ teaspoons salt or to taste
Freshly ground black pepper

1 fresh, hot green chili, finely chopped (do not remove seeds)
1 teaspoon store-bought garam masala (page 134)
A pinch of cayenne pepper
1½ tablespoons fresh lemon juice

Boil the potatoes with water to cover. When they are tender—this will take 15 to 20 minutes—drain and mash them with the back of a fork or a potato masher. Now add the hot milk and butter and beat with a whisk or a fork, adding 1 or 2 more tablespoons milk if needed for desired consistency. Add all the remaining ingredients and mix well.

The best way to keep mashed potatoes hot if you are not eating them right away is to place them in a covered double boiler.

SERVES 4–6

NEW POTATOES WITH CUMIN

Zeera aloo

∎∎∎∎∎∎∎

Here is one of my favorite ways of preparing small new potatoes, Indian-style. You may serve them with an Indian meal or, if you like, with Western dishes—anything from roasts to sausages. They are particularly good with my "Hamburger" Kebabs (page 27).

INGREDIENTS

2 pounds small new potatoes
1 teaspoon plus ¾ teaspoon salt
2½ tablespoons vegetable oil
1 teaspoon cumin seeds
1 teaspoon ground cumin

½ teaspoon store-bought garam masala *(page 134)*
⅛ to ¼ teaspoon cayenne pepper
2 to 3 tablespoons chopped fresh cilantro (Chinese parsley, fresh green coriander)

Scrub the potatoes and put them in a saucepan. Cover with water to come about 1 inch above the potatoes. Add 1 tablespoon salt to the water and bring to a boil. Cover and boil until the potatoes are just tender. Drain and peel.

Put the oil in a large frying pan and set over medium-high heat. When the oil is hot, put in the cumin seeds. Let the seeds sizzle for a few seconds. Now put in the potatoes. Turn the heat down to medium. Brown the potatoes lightly on all sides. Turn the heat to low and add ¾ teaspoon salt and the ground cumin, *garam masala,* and cayenne. Cook, stirring, for a minute. Add the cilantro just before serving and toss to mix.

SERVES 4–6

SIMPLY GRILLED TOMATOES

Grilled timatar

■ ■ ■ ■ ■ ■ ■

Sweet, juicy summer tomatoes are just perfect cooked this way. You will want to try them with your fried eggs as well as many of the chicken and fish dishes in this book.

I like to use two large tomatoes, but any size will do.

Ingredients

1¼ to 1½ pounds tomatoes	¼ teaspoon ground cumin
¼ teaspoon salt	A generous pinch of cayenne pepper
Freshly ground black pepper	2 teaspoons fresh lemon juice
¼ teaspoon store-bought garam masala *(page 134)*	2 teaspoons butter or olive oil *(optional)*

Preheat the grill.

Cut the tomatoes in halves crosswise. Sprinkle the salt, black pepper, *garam masala,* cumin, and cayenne over the cut surfaces and rub the spices in. Sprinkle the lemon juice on top and rub that in as well. Place under the hot grill, about 4 inches from the heat source and grill until the top is browned and the tomatoes are slightly limp. Dot with butter or dribble some oil over the top if you like.

SERVES 2–4

SPINACH WITH GINGER AND GREEN CHILIES

Saag bhaji

■ ■ ■ ■ ■ ■

Indians tend to eat a lot of greens, sometimes a single variety by itself, sometimes mixed with other leaves. The most commonly available of all greens in the West is spinach and that is what I have used here. Keep the leaves whole, but if they are very large you might need to chop them coarsely.

INGREDIENTS

1-inch piece fresh ginger, peeled	*About ½ teaspoon salt*
3 tablespoons vegetable oil	*½ teaspoon store-bought garam masala (page 134)*
1¼ pounds trimmed, washed spinach	*¼ teaspoon sugar*
2 to 3 fresh, hot green chilies, finely chopped (do not remove seeds)	*⅛ teaspoon cayenne pepper*

Cut the ginger, crosswise, into very thin slices. Stacking a few slices at a time together, cut them into very fine slivers.

Put the oil in a wok or large, wide pan and set over high heat. When the oil is very hot, put in the ginger. Stir until the ginger starts to brown. Put in the spinach and chilies. Stir and cook until the spinach has wilted completely. Add the salt, *garam masala,* sugar, and cayenne. Stir and cook for another 5 minutes.

SERVES 4

TURNIPS WITH CUMIN

Shorvedar shaljam

■■■■■■■

To this simple stew, you may add other vegetables such as potatoes, peas, carrots, or green beans. Serve it with rice or bread.

Ingredients

1 pound medium-sized turnips (about 5)	½ teaspoon cumin seeds
2 tablespoons chickpea flour (also called gram flour or besan)	2 to 3 hot, dried red chilies
5 canned plum tomatoes, well chopped, plus ⅓ cup juice from the can	⅛ teaspoon ground turmeric
	¾ teaspoon salt
2 tablespoons vegetable oil	

Peel the turnips and quarter them lengthwise. Turnips can have a rather thick skin. You should peel all of it away so that you will not be left with a coarse outer layer.

Put the chickpea flour in a bowl. Slowly add 2 tablespoons water, breaking up lumps as you go. Add the canned tomatoes, the juice from the can, and ¼ cup water. Set aside.

Put the oil in a medium-sized pan and set over medium-high heat. When the oil is hot, put in the cumin seeds. Stir once or twice and put in the red chilies. Stir once and put in the turnips and turmeric. Stir a few times and put in ½ cup water, the chickpea flour paste, and salt. Stir and bring to a boil. Cover, turn the heat to low and simmer for 15 to 20 minutes or until the turnips are tender.

Serves 4

BREAD AND RICE

■■■■■■■

Here are a few basic recipes to set you on your way. Plain rice cooks quickly anyway. If you add some herbs, spices, or vegetables, the cooking time may increase by a few minutes. Breads are more of a problem, as the dough needs to rest and then the breads have to be rolled out. But the bread I have included here cooks in less than a minute!

These days good Indian and Middle Eastern breads are sold by many supermarkets and take-out restaurants. To make your life easier, you can always buy these to eat with your delicious homemade chickpeas or chicken or lamb.

■■■■■■■

■■■■■■

■■■■■■

DEEP-FRIED PUFFY BREADS
Poori

■ ■ ■ ■ ■ ■

Pooris, for me, are the easiest of Indian breads and the first ones I teach in my cooking classes. Hence their inclusion in this chapter. These days you can always buy ready-made *naans* from Indian restaurants that have take-outs and pita breads from supermarkets. But *pooris* you do have to make yourself. They are quite heavenly when freshly prepared.

Chapati flour is sold by all Indian grocers. If you wish you can substitute a mixture of whole wheat and plain white flours.

INGREDIENTS

2 cups chapati *flour or a mixture of 1 cup sifted whole wheat flour and 1 cup all-purpose flour*
½ teaspoon salt

2 tablespoons vegetable oil plus more for deep-frying
7 to 8 tablespoons milk or water

Put the flour in a bowl. Add the salt and mix it in. Dribble the 2 tablespoons oil over the top and rub it into the flour with your fingers. Slowly add the milk or water to form a medium-soft ball of dough. Knead the dough for 10 minutes or until smooth. Form a smooth ball, rub it with a little oil, and set it aside, covered, for 15 to 30 minutes.

Just before eating, put enough oil for deep-frying into a wok or deep frying pan and set over medium heat. As it heats, divide the ball of dough into 12 balls. Roll one ball out into a 5-inch round. Keep it covered with plastic wrap. Roll out all the *pooris* this way and keep them covered. When the oil is very hot, lay one *poori* carefully over the surface of the oil without letting it fold up. It should sizzle immediately. Using the back of a slotted spoon, push the *poori* gently into the oil with quick strokes. It should puff up in seconds. Turn the *poori* over and cook on the second side for a few seconds. Remove with a slotted spoon and keep on a large plate lined with paper towels. Make all the *pooris* this way and eat immediately.

SERVES 3–4

PLAIN RICE

Saaday chaaval

■ ■ ■ ■ ■ ■

INGREDIENTS

2 cups long-grain white rice | *1 teaspoon salt, optional*

Put the rice in a bowl and wash well in several changes of water. Drain thoroughly.

In a heavy-bottomed saucepan, combine the rice, salt, and 2¾ cups water. Bring to a boil. Cover tightly, turn the heat to very, very low, and cook for 25 minutes.

SERVES 4–6

TURMERIC RICE

Peelay chaaval

■ ■ ■ ■ ■ ■

This yellow, lightly seasoned rice may be served with almost any Indian meal.

INGREDIENTS

2 cups basmati rice	*1-inch stick cinnamon*
3 tablespoons vegetable oil	*2 cloves garlic, peeled and finely chopped*
3 whole cloves	*¼ teaspoon ground turmeric*
1 bay leaf	*1 teaspoon salt*
4 cardamom pods	*2 tablespoons finely sliced chives or the green part of green onions*

Put the rice in a bowl and wash well in several changes of water. Drain and leave in a strainer set over a bowl.

Put the oil in a heavy saucepan and set over medium-high heat. When the oil is hot, put in the cloves, bay leaf, cardamom pods, and cinnamon. Stir once or twice and put in the garlic. As soon as the garlic turns medium brown, put in the rice, turmeric, and salt. Stir gently for a minute. Now put in 2¾ cups water and bring to a boil. Cover tightly, turn the heat down very, very low, and cook for 25 minutes. Sprinkle with chives before serving.

SERVES 4–6

RICE WITH MUSHROOMS AND MUSTARD SEEDS

Khumbi chaaval

■■■■■■

Almost any variety of fresh, seasonal mushrooms may be used here. Ordinary white ones also work perfectly well.

INGREDIENTS

2 cups long-grain white rice	1 slice (1 ounce) onion, peeled and cut into fine half rings
3 tablespoons vegetable oil	10 medium-sized fresh mushrooms, sliced lengthwise
½ teaspoon cumin seeds	2¾ cups chicken stock or water
½ teaspoon black or yellow mustard seeds	½ to 1 teaspoon salt

Put the rice in a bowl and wash well in several changes of water. Drain and leave in a strainer set over a bowl.

Put the oil in a heavy saucepan and set over medium-high heat. When the oil is hot, put in the cumin and mustard seeds. As soon as the mustard seeds begin to pop—this takes just a few seconds—put in the onion. Stir and fry until the onion browns a little. Put in the mushrooms and stir for a minute. Now put in the drained rice and stir for a minute. Put in the stock and about ½ teaspoon salt if your stock is salted, 1 teaspoon salt if you are using water or unsalted stock. Bring to a boil. Cover tightly, turn the heat to very, very low, and cook for 25 minutes.

SERVES 4–5

RICE WITH PEAS AND DILL

Matar aur sooay ka pullao

■ ■ ■ ■ ■ ■ ■

This dish is just as good for the family as it is for dinner guests.

INGREDIENTS

2 cups basmati rice

3 tablespoons vegetable oil

3 whole cloves

4 cardamom pods

1 small onion (4 ounces), peeled and cut into half rings

1 or 2 teaspoons salt, the lesser quantity if you are using unsalted stock or water

1 teaspoon store-bought or homemade garam masala *(page 134)*

¼ cup finely chopped fresh dill or 1½ tablespoons dried dill

2¾ cups chicken stock or water

1 cup shelled fresh or frozen peas, cooked for just 2 minutes in boiling water

Put the rice in a bowl and wash well in several changes of water. Drain and leave in a strainer set over a bowl.

Put the oil in a heavy saucepan and set over medium-high heat. When the oil is hot, put in the cloves and cardamom pods. Stir for a few seconds. Put in the onion. Stir until the onion is brown. Put in the rice, 1 teaspoon salt, *garam masala*, and dill. Stir for a minute. Now put in the stock and the second teaspoon salt if needed, and bring to a boil. Cover very tightly, turn the heat to very, very low, and cook for 20 minutes. Put in the peas. Cook for another 5 to 7 minutes. Stir gently before serving.

SERVES 5–6

SALADS, RELISHES, CHUTNEYS, AND PICKLES

■ ■ ■ ■ ■ ■ ■

India has a whole world of little salads, relishes, chutneys, and pickles. No meal is considered complete without at least one such offering to perk it up. Not only do these offerings add tiny bits of concentrated flavor to a meal, but also they add vitamins. They are taken for granted and appear without being asked for. Sometimes they can be as simple as finely sliced red onions and tomatoes sprinkled with salt, pepper, and lemon juice or they can be pickles that take a few days to mature.

Every home has its own tradition of preparing carrot pickle with brown sugar, for example, or putting curry leaves into mango pickle, or making mango chutney with a particular combination of spices. I have included one very special mango chutney here: Fresh Green Mango Chutney (page 111). It was made by my mother in the hot summer months and is quite extraordinary. It is also quick and easy to prepare.

■ ■ ■ ■ ■ ■ ■

■■■■■■■

■■■■■■■

FRESH TOMATO SALAD

Timatar ka salad

■■■■■■

This tastes best when tomatoes are in season. The addition of fresh basil leaves is a quirky preference of mine, mainly because they grow in such abundance in my garden and look so pretty. You could just as easily tuck in sprigs of fresh mint or cilantro.

INGREDIENTS

1½ pounds tomatoes	*2 tablespoons fresh lemon juice*
20 to 25 fresh basil or mint leaves	*3 tablespoons vegetable oil (I use a mixture of 2 tablespoons*
½ teaspoon salt	*peanut oil and 1 tablespoon mustard oil)*
Freshly ground black pepper	*½ teaspoon cumin seeds*
⅛ to ¼ teaspoon cayenne pepper	*½ teaspoon black or yellow mustard seeds*

Cut the tomatoes into ¼-inch slices and arrange in slightly overlapping layers on a large plate. Tuck the basil or mint leaves singly into the layers of tomatoes so that about three-quarters of each leaf is visible. Do this evenly so that the green and red are prettily distributed. Sprinkle the salt, black pepper, cayenne, and lemon juice over the tomatoes. Put the oil in a small saucepan and set over high heat. When the oil is hot, put in the cumin and mustard seeds. As soon as the mustard seeds begin to pop—this takes just a few seconds—lift the saucepan off the heat and spoon the oil and spices over the tomatoes, being careful to avoid the leaves. Serve immediately.

SERVES 4–6

YOGURT WITH TOMATO AND CUCUMBER

Timatar aur kheeray ka raita

■ ■ ■ ■ ■ ■

A cooling delight, perfect for hot, spicy meals or for eating by itself.

INGREDIENTS

2 cups plain yogurt
½ to ¾ teaspoon salt
Freshly ground black pepper
⅛ teaspoon cayenne pepper

½ teaspoon ground roasted cumin seeds (page 133)
1 small tomato, cut into small dice
About 4-inch piece cucumber, peeled and cut into small dice

Put the yogurt into a bowl. Beat lightly with a fork until smooth. Add all the remaining ingredients and mix well.

SERVES 4–6

YOGURT WITH CARROT AND GOLDEN RAISINS

Gajar au kishmish ka raita

■ ■ ■ ■ ■ ■

The taste of this takes me back to the hundreds of festive banquets I have attended where something of this sort—a sweet-and-sour relish—always accompanied the main meal. You may serve it in small, individual bowls, if you like. In that case a teaspoon would be the best eating implement. It could also be served at the end of a family meal as a salad-cum-dessert.

INGREDIENTS

1¼ cups plain yogurt
½ teaspoon sugar
¼ teaspoon salt
¼ teaspoon cayenne pepper
1 medium-sized carrot, peeled and coarsely grated

1 tablespoon vegetable oil
¼ teaspoon cumin seeds
¼ teaspoon black or yellow mustard seeds
2 tablespoons golden raisins

Put the yogurt into a bowl. Beat lightly with a fork until smooth and creamy. Add the sugar, salt, chili powder, and carrot. Mix.

Put the oil in a very small frying pan and set over medium-high heat. When the oil is very hot, put in the cumin seeds and mustard seeds. As soon as the mustard seeds begin to pop—this just takes a few seconds—put in the raisins. Stir once and empty the contents of the frying pan—oil and all—over the bowl of yogurt. Mix.

SERVES 4

FRESH GREEN MANGO CHUTNEY

Aam ki lonji

■ ■ ■ ■ ■ ■

I had forgotten about this summer delight altogether. It was not until my sister Lalit in London made it that I remembered how much I had loved it as a child. Memories of breakfasts and lunches with fresh *pooris*, vegetables, and this chutney came flooding back. I realized that I had not eaten it for almost twenty years. I hope you love it as much as I do.

Now, you do need green, unripe mangoes for this. These are not just hard mangoes that are destined to be ready for the table in a few days but really unripe ones whose entire flesh has a greenish tinge and is quite sour. They are sold, in season—which probably lasts from April until July, though produce from the southern hemisphere may make it last longer—by Indian grocers and come in all sizes, from fist-sized or even smaller to the size (but not the shape) of a hefty melon. Just ask for the mangoes used to make chutneys and pickles.

For this recipe I used one very large mango that weighed about 1½ pounds. It had one rather slim stone so the weight of the flesh after peeling and removing the stone was a little more than 1 pound. After cutting the flesh into strips, I was able to fill a quart jar almost to capacity. Because of the variation in available mango sizes, perhaps this is what you should aim for.

This chutney may be served with any meal, Indian or Western. Stored in a closed jar in the refrigerator it should keep for a couple of weeks—if you do not eat it up first. My recipe is for a mild chutney. If you want it hotter, increase the cayenne. Mangoes vary in their sourness, so do taste the chutney a good 5 minutes before it is ready and adjust the sugar and salt, if necessary.

INGREDIENTS

½ teaspoon fenugreek seeds

1½ to 2 pounds green, unripe mangoes (see recipe introduction)

¼ cup mustard oil (page 135), or olive oil as a substitute

½ teaspoon cumin seeds

½ teaspoon fennel seeds

½ teaspoon black or yellow mustard seeds

¼ teaspoon kalonji seeds (page 135)

2½-inch piece fresh ginger, peeled and cut into slivers

¼ teaspoon ground turmeric

1 to 1¼ teaspoons salt

5 to 6 tablespoons sugar

3 to 4 fresh, hot green chilies

½ teaspoon cayenne pepper

Soak the fenugreek seeds in ⅓ cup water overnight.

Peel the mango and cut the flesh off the stone. Cut into strips that are ¼-inch thick and wide and 2 to 3 inches long. If you are in a rush, chop the flesh coarsely.

Set the oil in a heavy saucepan over medium-high heat. When the oil is hot, put in the cumin, fennel, mustard, and kalonji seeds. As soon as the mustard seeds begin to pop—this takes just a few seconds—put in the ginger. Stir and fry it for 2 minutes or until it just starts to change color. Now put in the soaked fenugreek seeds with their soaking liquid as well as another 1 cup water and the turmeric. Bring to a boil. Cover, lower the heat, and simmer for 15 minutes. Add the mango, salt, sugar, green chilies, and cayenne. Stir to mix and bring to a simmer. Simmer, uncovered, on medium-low heat for 25 to 30 minutes or until the chutney is thick and all the mango pieces are translucent and tender. Serve at room temperature.

MAKES ABOUT 2½ CUPS

FRESH GREEN CHUTNEY

Hari chutney

■ ■ ■ ■ ■ ■

This chutney may be served with all Indian meals. It goes particularly well with Onion Fritters (page 20) and Indian Mashed Potatoes (page 90).

INGREDIENTS

6 tablespoons plain yogurt
2 heaping tablespoons coarsely chopped mint
2 heaping tablespoons coarsely chopped fresh cilantro (Chinese parsley, fresh green coriander)

1 tablespoon fresh lemon juice
⅓ teaspoon salt or to taste

Put 2 tablespoons of the yogurt and the mint, cilantro, lemon juice, and salt into the container of an electric blender and blend until smooth, pushing down with a rubber spatula if necessary.

Put the remaining 4 tablespoons of yogurt into a bowl and beat lightly. Add the paste from the blender. Stir to mix.

This chutney may be stored, covered, in the refrigerator for 2 to 3 days.

SERVES 6

FRESH RED CHUTNEY WITH ALMONDS

Lal chutney

■ ■ ■ ■ ■ ■

This is the chutney that is traditionally served with "Hamburger" Kebabs (page 27). I now like it so much I serve it with most of my meals.

Instead of fresh, hot red chilies, I have used a combination of red bell pepper and cayenne pepper. You may use the former, if you wish. It will be much hotter. Also, walnuts may be used instead of the almonds. Both would be traditional and authentic.

This chutney may be kept in the refrigerator (well covered) for a few days.

INGREDIENTS

½ large red bell pepper, seeded and coarsely chopped
20 large fresh mint leaves or 30 smaller ones, coarsely chopped
2 tablespoons fresh lemon juice
1 clove garlic, peeled and coarsely chopped
½ teaspoon cayenne pepper

½ teaspoon salt
Freshly ground black pepper
1 tablespoon blanched, chopped, or slivered almonds
1 teaspoon chopped dill, optional

Into the container of an electric blender, put the red pepper, mint, lemon juice, garlic, cayenne, salt, and black pepper in the order listed. Blend until smooth. Add the almonds and blend again. A few bits of almonds can be left unpulverized. Pour into a bowl and check for seasonings. You may now mix in the dill, if you wish.

SERVES 8

CARROT AND GREEN BEAN PICKLE

Gajar aur sem ka achar

■ ■ ■ ■ ■ ■ ■

No Indian meal is complete without a proper pickle to offer its unique brand of piquancy. Of course you could buy it ready-made from an Indian grocer. But mass-produced pickles seem to suffer from a sameness of taste. This scrumptious, mustardy pickle—an invention of mine—is like no other and is quick and easy to prepare as well. It does, however, take several days to mature, but these are days when minimum effort is required: All you have to do is shake the jar a few times. It may be served with all Indian meals. You could also serve small amounts with Western foods such as roast chicken or leg of lamb, or even with grilled sausages and baked hams.

INGREDIENTS

5 tablespoons black or yellow mustard seeds	4 ounces green beans, trimmed at the ends
2 tablespoons coriander seeds	2 medium-sized carrots (about 3 ounces each), trimmed and peeled
1½ teaspoons cayenne pepper	3 tablespoons fresh lemon juice
1 teaspoon salt	5 tablespoons corn or peanut oil
½ teaspoon ground turmeric	

Put the mustard seeds into the container of a spice grinder or clean coffee grinder and grind very coarsely for just a few seconds. Empty into a glass or stainless steel bowl. Put the coriander seeds into the same grinder and grind a little more finely—to a coarse powder. Put into the same bowl. Add the cayenne, salt, and turmeric. Mix with a stainless steel spoon.

Do not wash the green beans. Just wipe them with a lightly dampened cloth, if necessary. Cut the beans into halves, lengthwise, and then into 2-inch segments. Cut the carrots, crosswise, into 2-inch pieces and then into sticks the same size as the beans. Add the beans and carrots, as well as the lime juice, to the spices in the bowl. Mix well and put into a 1-quart glass jar with a plastic lid. Place the closed jar in a sunny window for 4 days, shaking it a few times each day.

Heat the oil in a small saucepan until it is smoking and then allow it to cool thoroughly. Pour the cooled oil over the beans and carrots. Shake well. The pickle is now ready to be eaten. Tightly sealed and refrigerated, it will keep for about a year.

MAKES 3 TO 4 CUPS

DRINKS AND DESSERTS

■■■■■■■

Indians generally end their meals with fresh fruit, of which we have an abundance: litchis, loquats, *chikoos* (sapote, *chikozapote*), jackfruit, star fruit, custard apples, strawberries, cherries, melons, mangoes, guavas, pineapples, to say nothing of oranges, tangerines, apples, and dozens of types of banana. Some people like to end their meals with a little plain yogurt, salted or mixed with a little sugar. Our sweets—they should be called sweetmeats or candies—are really eaten at teatime or at banquets.

In this chapter I have included yogurt drinks and some simple *halvas* and fruit-based desserts. Many Indians like to serve cut-up fresh fruit, such as apples, bananas and oranges, with a simple English custard, a trick I am sure they learned from the British. I was brought up on this and so have included it here, though I am sure you have your own favorite custard recipe.

■■■■■■■

■■■■■■■

■■■■■■■

PALE GREEN, SPICY, MINTY LASSI

Hari lassi

■ ■ ■ ■ ■ ■

I cannot think of anything more refreshing for a hot summer day.

INGREDIENTS

1¼ cups plain yogurt
3 tablespoons chopped fresh cilantro (Chinese parsley, fresh green coriander)
25 large fresh mint leaves or 30 smaller ones
½-inch piece fresh ginger, peeled and chopped

½ fresh, hot green chili (use the upper half for more heat, the lower for less), coarsely chopped (do not remove seeds)
⅓ teaspoon salt or to taste
¼ teaspoon ground roasted cumin seeds (page 133), optional
8 ice cubes

Combine all the ingredients in an electric blender and blend until smooth. Some ice pieces may remain. Pour into 2 glasses and serve.

SERVES 2

SWEET, PALE ORANGE, MANGO LASSI
Aam ki lassi

■■■■■■

Soothing and satisfying, this could be made with peeled, fresh, ripe mangoes or with good canned ones. Drain the canned mangoes before using them.

INGREDIENTS

1¼ cups plain yogurt
1 cup chopped, ripe mango
3 tablespoons sugar or to taste

¼ teaspoon ground cardamom seeds (page 132)
8 ice cubes

Combine all the ingredients in an electric blender and blend. Some ice pieces may remain. Pour into 2 or 3 glasses and serve.

SERVES 2–3

FRESH FRUIT WITH CUSTARD

Custard may taazay phal

■ ■ ■ ■ ■ ■

When we lived with my grandfather, all forty or so of his children and grandchildren, this was our most common dessert. Fresh fruit, mainly the apples, tangerines, and bananas that we saw through much of the winter, were sliced and mixed in with cool homemade custard. I am sure it was easy to prepare then and it remains easy now.

I have used just oranges and bananas. The bananas should be sliced at the last minute.

INGREDIENTS

Custard	*Fruit*
2 cups milk	2 oranges
4 egg yolks	2 bananas
7 tablespoons sugar	
1½ teaspoons vanilla extract	

Heat the milk in a heavy saucepan until very hot.

Beat the egg yolks in a bowl with a whisk until smooth. Slowly add the sugar as you continue to beat the mixture. Stop only when it is pale yellow and thick. Now slowly pour in the very hot milk, beating as you go. Pour this egg and milk mixture back into the saucepan and set over medium-low heat, stirring all the time until it has thickened but not boiled. Boiling will curdle it. Remove from the heat and pour into a fresh, cool bowl immediately. Stir for a bit as it cools. When cool, add the vanilla extract and mix. Cover and refrigerate until needed.

Peel the oranges with a knife so that no white pith remains. Cut into ⅓-inch-thick round slices. Now cut each slice into 6 even wedges. Peel the bananas and slice them into ⅓-inch rounds. In a large bowl, mix the custard with the fruit. Divide among 4 smaller bowls and serve.

SERVES 4

CARAMELIZED CARDAMOM APPLES WITH PISTACHIO CREAM

Sev ka murabba

■ ■ ■ ■ ■ ■

An easy dessert that can be made with any sour, firm apples such as Granny Smiths. It may be served hot or warm.

INGREDIENTS

Cream
1 cup heavy, whipping cream
2 tablespoons unsalted pistachios, finely chopped

Apples
¼ pound (1 stick) unsalted butter
4 medium-sized sour, firm apples

¼ teaspoon finely ground cardamom seeds (page 132)
⅛ teaspoon ground cinnamon
⅛ teaspoon ground cloves
⅔ cup sugar
3 tablespoons blanched, slivered almonds
2 tablespoons chopped walnuts

Whip the cream lightly in a bowl until it just holds its shape but is not stiff at all. Fold half of the pistachio nuts into the cream, cover, and refrigerate.

Melt the butter over low heat in a large, nonstick frying pan. Take the pan off the heat. Peel, core, and slice the apples thinly, dropping the slices into the butter as you cut them. Fold them into the butter as you go so that they do not discolor. (You could, if you like, keep the frying pan over very low heat as you do this.) Add the cardamom, cinnamon, cloves, sugar, almonds, and walnuts. Cook on medium heat for 2 to 3 minutes, stirring gently as you do so. Now turn the heat to high. Cook for 8 to 10 minutes, stirring very gently now and then, until the apples have caramelized lightly.

Serve on individual plates with a dollop of the cream partially on and partially off the apples. Sprinkle the remaining chopped pistachios over the cream.

SERVES 4

BANANA HALVA
Kelay ka halva
■ ■ ■ ■ ■ ■

If you love bananas in all forms, as I do, you will love this simple but unusual preparation. I often form the *halva,* which is quite malleable, into fig shapes and serve it on individual plates with whipped cream. The *halva* will keep, unrefrigerated, for a couple of days. Just wrap it well in plastic wrap.

INGREDIENTS

4 very ripe bananas	*1 tablespoon chopped, unsalted, peeled pistachios*
1 tablespoon vegetable oil or ghee *(page 135)*	*½ tablespoon chopped walnuts*
2 tablespoons sugar	*¼ cup lightly whipped heavy cream or clotted cream*

Peel the bananas and mash them.

Put the oil or *ghee* in a nonstick frying pan and set over medium–high heat. When the oil is hot, put in the mashed bananas. Stir and fry for 5 to 6 minutes. Turn the heat to medium and stir and fry for another 10 minutes or until the bananas have browned and turned to a kind of soft toffee. Turn the heat to low. Add the sugar. Stir for another 30 seconds or until the sugar has dissolved. Add the pistachios and walnuts and mix in. Cool to room temperature, then cover with plastic wrap until serving time. Serve with whipped or clotted cream.

SERVES 2–4

WHOLE WHEAT FLOUR HALVA

Attey ka halva

■ ■ ■ ■ ■ ■

This *halva* is generally made with *chapati* flour, sold by all Indian grocers, but you could easily make it with ordinary whole wheat flour. The important thing to watch for is the frying of the flour. It should turn toffee colored before any liquid is added or it will taste raw.

The traditional proportions of flour, sugar, oil, and water for this halva are 1, ¾ , ¾, 2 by volume. You can increase or decrease the amounts as long as you keep to these proportions. *Ghee* instead of oil makes a richer *halva*.

INGREDIENTS

1½ cups sugar	*2 cups whole wheat or* chapati *flour*
Seeds from 4 cardamom pods	*2 to 3 tablespoons mixed, chopped, blanched almonds and*
1½ cups vegetable oil or ghee *(page 135)*	*unsalted pistachios*

Put the sugar in a medium-sized saucepan. Add 4 cups water and bring to a simmer. Throw in the seeds from the cardamom pods. Cook until the sugar has dissolved, which will take a minute or two. Set this syrup aside.

Put the oil or *ghee* in a large, wide, preferably nonstick saucepan and set over medium-high heat. When the oil is hot, add the flour. Turn the heat down to medium. Stir and fry until the flour turns a warm toffee color. This will take about 8 minutes. Add the syrup, stirring as you go. The syrup will make the *halva* bubble up. Keep stirring, turning the heat down if necessary, until the *halva* has thickened—a matter of a few minutes. Add the nuts and mix them in. Turn off the heat and serve warm. (This *halva* may easily be reheated in a microwave oven.)

SERVES 4–5

MENUS

■■■■■■■

A Simple Lunch
Gingery Cauliflower Soup (page 11)
French or Italian bread
A green salad

■

A Quick Bite Before or After the Theater
"Hamburger" Kebabs (page 27)
Store-bought naan or pita bread
Fresh Green Chutney (page 113)
Fresh Red Chutney with Almonds (page 114)

■

A One-Pot Meal
Chicken, Red Lentils, and Green Beans in One Pot (page 58)
Plain Rice (page 100) or any bread
A green salad

■

A Family Meal
Fried Fish Steaks (page 67)
Indian Mashed Potatoes (page 90) or plain boiled potatoes
Spinach with Ginger and Green Chilies (page 94)

■

Teatime
Onion Fritters (page 20)
Fresh Green Chutney (page 113)
Tea

■

Sunday Breakfast or Brunch
Garlicky Mushroom Masala Omelet (page 43)
Toast or French bread
Tea or coffee

ENTERTAINING GOOD FRIENDS
The Most Delicious Meat Cubes (page 29)
Rice with Peas and Dill (page 103)
Fresh fruit

■

ENTERTAINING MORE GOOD FRIENDS
Silken Chicken (page 46)
Turmeric Rice (page 100)
Gently Stewed Beets (page 85)

■

SIMPLE FAMILY SUPPER
Hard-Boiled Eggs Masala (page 41)
Rice with Mushrooms and Mustard Seeds (page 102)

■

SATURDAY DINNER
Smothered Lamb (or Pork or Beef) (page 31)
Rice with Peas and Dill (page 103)
Yogurt with Tomato and Cucumber (page 108)

■

A VEGETARIAN MEAL
Red Lentils Tarka (page 80)
Plain Rice (page 100) or Deep-Fried Puffy Breads (page 99)
Cauliflower with Ginger, Garlic, and Green Chilies (page 83)
Plain yogurt

■

A CLASSIC MEAL
Beef or Lamb with Spinach (page 36)
Store-bought naan *or pita bread*
Fresh Tomato Salad (page 107)

A COCKTAIL PARTY
Shrimp with Garlic and Chilies (page 17)
Delicious Chicken Bits (page 14)

■

AN ELEGANT PRAWN MEAL
Stir-Fried Shrimp in an Aromatic Tomato-Cream Sauce (page 70)
Plain Rice (page 100)
A green salad

■

A PICNIC MENU
Delicious Chicken Bits (page 14)
Curried Tuna (page 63)
French bread or pita bread
Fresh Tomato Salad (page 107)
Chilled white wine

■

ENTERTAINING IN THE SUMMER
A Light, Cold Yogurt Soup (page 12)
Chicken Breasts Baked with Green Chilies and Onions (page 55)
Green Peas in a Creamy Sauce (page 87)
Plain Rice (page 100)
Fresh fruit such as chilled mangoes

■

ENTERTAINING IN THE WINTER
Pork or Lamb Vindaloo (page 33)
Stir-Fried Green Cabbage with Fennel Seeds (page 88)
Plain Rice (page 100)
Caramelized Cardamom Apples with Pistachio Cream (page 122)

UTENSILS
∎∎∎∎∎∎∎

No extra-special utensils are needed for preparing Indian meals, but it does help to have the following:

WOK OR *Karhai*

A *karhai* is just an Indian wok. It tends to be a bit more rounded but performs the same function as the wok. Both are half-moon shaped and both are excellent for deep-frying and stir-frying. Slightly rounded spatulas that best-fit the wok's shape are also useful.

ELECTRIC BLENDER OR FOOD PROCESSOR OR BOTH

In India, a grinding stone is used for grinding garlic, onions, and ginger. Electric machines are less romantic but also less wearing on the body. They work fast. One very useful way of finely chopping onions, garlic, or ginger involves throwing them into a food processor and then starting and stopping the machine with great rapidity until the desired result is achieved. This is known as the pulse method.

COFFEE GRINDER

Dry spices cannot be ground in blenders or food processors. Only a clean coffee grinder will do. I keep an extra one for the purpose. Just wipe it off with a dry or very lightly dampened cloth when you are finished with it.

PRESSURE COOKER

A pressure cooker is necessary only for speed. Meats such as beef, lamb, and pork will not stew quickly any other way. Of all the pressure cookers I tested, the one I liked the best—it really made cooking a breeze—was a Duromatic Pressure Cooker made by Kuhn-Rikon Corp., P.O. Box 1184, Enfield, CT 06083-1184; telephone (203) 244-2300; fax (203) 246-2217. It comes in many shapes and sizes. I have the one that resembles a frying pan. The bottom of these pans, even though they are all stainless steel, is virtually nonstick and the opening and closing mechanisms work as if they had been freshly oiled. There is no separate weight that has to be placed on the top and no frightening, hissing noises as the cooking proceeds. A truly wonderful gadget.

NONSTICK PANS

I like nonstick pans. They make my cooking easier. The heavier the pan, the better the quality usually is. Pans with the same brand name may come in different weights. Look for the one that is the heaviest. Nowadays, one can find pans in which the nonstick element is so well bonded to the bottom metal that the two are inseparable. These are ideal. Use wooden or plastic spatulas and spoons when cooking with these pans so that you do not scratch the nonstick surface.

TONGS

Tongs come in very handy when you need to turn pieces of meat over or pick up grilled or fried chicken pieces, or when you need to delve into a sauce to remove, say, a bay leaf. Make sure the tongs move easily before you buy them. Stiff tongs are virtually useless.

GINGER GRATER

A ginger grater looks like an ordinary grater but has no holes or openings. It can only be found in stores that sell Asian cooking utensils and is generally made in Japan. Some Japanese grocers sell them. I find that I just cannot do without my ginger grater. It grates ginger to a pulp in seconds and, what is best, holds the rough fibers back while allowing me to collect the pulp.

TECHNIQUES
■■■■■■■

HOW TO PEEL AND CLEAN SHRIMP

Most shrimp available in the West already have their heads removed. But if yours don't, first pull the head off. Now, pull off the dangling feet. Peel the shell, which should come away in rings. Pull away the shell on the tail. Make a shallow cut along the back of the prawn and remove the vein. Put all the cleaned shrimp in a bowl. Rub with 1 to 2 tablespoons coarse or kosher salt. Wash the shrimp. Rub with salt once more and then wash well and drain. Pat the shrimp dry and store in a well-closed plastic bag in the refrigerator until you are ready to cook.

HOW TO PREPARE AND CLEAN SQUID

Twist the head (with the tentacles) off. Cut off the hard area near the eyes but retain the head. Squeeze or pull out all the soft tissue still left inside the tubular body as well as the hard cartilagelike "pen." Peel off the fine skin on the tubular body. Now wash both the body and the head with salt as suggested for the shrimp. Drain and pat dry. Store as suggested for the shrimp.

MAKING YOGURT SALAD

Always beat yogurt lightly with a whisk or fork until it is smooth and creamy *before* adding cucumbers, onions, or any other solid ingredients. This is particularly necessary for homemade yogurt, which will be somewhat lumpy if it is not whisked.

DEEP-FRYING

Make sure that the oil is hot enough before you add the ingredients to be fried. If a medium-low or medium temperature is called for, set the heat to that temperature and wait 5 to 7 minutes for the oil to heat up. Then put in a small piece of bread. If it begins to sizzle immediately, the oil is ready for deep-frying.

Tarka: THE TECHNIQUE OF FRYING WHOLE SPICES IN HOT OIL

In China, cut green onions are dropped into a little hot oil and the combination is dribbled over a freshly steamed fish. In parts of the Mediterranean region, similar effects are achieved with olive oil and garlic. In India, we would call this technique *tarka* or *baghaar*. We might use quite a few spices and seasonings to achieve a more complex result. Dishes in Indian can be given both a final flavoring or an initial flavoring by heating oil and then, when it is very hot, putting in whole spices such as cumin seeds or mustard seeds. The spices are allowed to sizzle and pop for a few seconds. Foods such as small boiled potatoes or raw cauliflower pieces are then added to the pan to be stir-fried, or the contents of the pan—oil and spices—are poured over, say, a dish of cooked legumes.

AN INDIAN PANTRY
■■■■■■■

AJWAIN SEEDS

These small seeds look rather like celery seeds and are sold only by Indian grocers. In this cookbook, I have replaced them with dried thyme or oregano, as their aroma lies somewhat between the two. If you manage to get *ajwain,* use only half the quantity, as it is quite strong.

ASAFETIDA

A brownish resin of strong odor, *asafetida* is used to give a special kick to Indian foods. Even though used in small quantities, it subtly transforms the taste of a dish. It also happens to be a digestive. The ground variety is easy to use.

BASMATI RICE

Now quite readily available, basmati rice is long-grained and quite aromatic. For best texture, it should be washed before being used, even though many packagers suggest otherwise.

BLACK PEPPER

It is best to buy black pepper in bulk. Major Indian grocers sell it in 1-pound and 5-pound bags. Store it in closed canisters in a dark, cool place. Bought from supermarkets in small jars, it is much more expensive.

CARDAMOM

A highly aromatic spice, cardamom is generally sold in its pod form. Indians like to use the green pods but most supermarkets seem to stock the bleached, less aromatic whitish pods. Use whatever you can get. If cardamom *seeds* are called for, either remove them from their pods or buy them loose from an Indian grocer. To grind small amounts of cardamom seeds, use a mortar and pestle. When cardamom pods are used whole, they should not be eaten.

CAYENNE PEPPER

This is the ground version of dried red chilies.

CHAPATI FLOUR

This is a very finely ground whole wheat flour sold only by Indian grocers. The best substitute for *chapati* flour is a mixture of whole wheat and all-purpose flour in equal proportions.

Chickpea Flour

Also known as gram flour and *besan* in Indian shops and *farine de pois chiches* in French and other specialty shops. Chickpea flour is made from ground, dried chickpeas. I store mine in the refrigerator to discourage bugs.

Chickpeas (Garbanzo Beans)

Because dried chickpeas take a long time to soak and cook, I have used only canned ones (often labeled garbanzo beans) in this book. Drain the chickpeas well and rinse them again before using. This gets rid of their "tinny" taste.

Chilies

The chili peppers I use tend to be slim and about 2 to 4 inches long and of the cayenne variety. They are generally green, but when they ripen they can turn red. The hottest part is at the stem end where there are a lot of seeds. Chilies tend to vary in their heat. Wear gloves or wash your hands carefully after cutting them.

Dried red peppers are the same chilies, ripened and dried. I generally use them whole to lessen their heat but to take advantage of their flavor.

Cilantro (Chinese Parsley, Fresh Green Coriander)

A very popular herb in India, where it is called green coriander. To store cilantro, put it, roots first, into a tall glass of water. Cover with a plastic bag and keep in the refrigerator. When a few tablespoons are called for, pull off a handful of leaves and tender stems from the top, wash and pat dry, and then chop as the recipe requires.

Coconut Milk

For the purposes of this quick and easy book, I have not suggested freshly made coconut milk. Canned coconut milk is just fine but use only a good-quality brand. The milk should be creamy white and not oily. A brand I like is Chaokoh, a product of Thailand. This is sold in Indian and Southeast Asian stores. Unless suggested otherwise, stir the milk well before use, as the cream tends to rise to the top.

Cumin Seeds, Whole and Ground

Shaped rather like caraway seeds, cumin seeds, in their whole and ground forms, are used with great frequency in Indian cooking. Both forms are sold by supermarkets and Indian grocers. *To make ground roasted cumin seeds:* Put 4 to 5 tablespoons of the whole seeds into a small cast-iron frying pan and set over medium heat. Stir the seeds and roast them over dry heat until they turn a few shades darker and emit a wonderful roasted aroma. Wait for them to cool slightly and then grind them in a clean coffee or spice grinder. Store in a tightly closed jar. This is a useful spice to have on hand. It will last a good month or two, through its flavor will gradually fade.

Black cumin seeds are finer than regular cumin seeds and much more expensive. I use them to make my own *garam masala*.

CURRY LEAVES

These highly aromatic leaves are best when fresh. Many Indian grocers sell them. Curry leaves are shaped like bay leaves but are much smaller. Many leaves are attached to a single stem and can be removed easily with one fluid movement of the fingers along the stalk. They can be stored in the refrigerator in a plastic bag. They can also be stored in the freezer the same way. Do this while they are still fresh and green. They may then go straight from freezer to pan.

CURRY POWDER

In the interests of speed, I have turned to a rather good brand of curry powder, Bolst's. I like their hot curry powder. You may use any brand you like.

FENNEL SEEDS

Shaped like cumin seeds but plumper and greener, fennel seeds have an aniselike flavor.

FENUGREEK SEEDS

Yellowish and squarish, fenugreek seeds give curry powder its special odor.

GARAM MASALA

My own recipe for this spice mixture requires 1 tablespoon cardamom seeds, a 2-inch cinnamon stick, one-third of a nutmeg, and 1 teaspoon *each* black peppercorns, black cumin seeds, and whole cloves, all thrown into a clean coffee or spice grinder and ground to a powder. However, to make matters easier, I have mostly suggested the use of store-bought *garam masala*. All Indian grocers sell it. When a recipe calls for the store-bought version, *do not* use my recipe, even if you have some on hand. The tastes are quite different.

GHEE

This is butter that has been clarified so thoroughly that you can even deep-fry in it. As no milk solids remain, *ghee* does not need refrigeration. It has a nutty, buttery taste. All Indian grocers sell it.

GINGER, FRESH

Ginger is a knobby, brown-skinned rhizome. It should be peeled before being used. When I refer to a 1-inch or 2-inch piece of ginger, just take that much off the length of the rhizome. Do not worry about the width. When very fine slivers are required, cut the peeled ginger, crosswise, into very fine slices. Then, stacking a few slices together, cut lengthwise into very fine strips. When "ginger grated to a pulp" is required, peel as much ginger as is called for, but do not cut the peeled section off the main rhizome. Using the main rhizome as a handle, grate the peeled ginger on the finest part of the grater to get a soft pulp. The Japanese sell special graters for ginger. Get one if you can.

KALONJI SEEDS

Small, tear-shaped, black seeds sold by Indian grocers, *kalonji* seeds have a carrotlike flavor.

MUSTARD

The mustard I have used in this book is a substitute for mustard seeds ground in vinegar. It is a coarse, grainy French mustard that is labeled Pommery *Moutarde de Meaux.* Dijon mustard is generally smooth and is easily available.

MUSTARD OIL

This is a wonderful oil. Get to know it. The best substitute for mustard oil is a fruity olive oil. The flavors are quite different but the richness is similar.

MUSTARD SEEDS, BLACK

These are sometimes black, sometimes reddish brown. The yellow mustard seeds sold by most supermarkets may be used as a substitute.

To grind mustard seeds: Just put them into a clean coffee or spice grinder and grind very briefly.

RED LENTILS

Known as *masoor dal* in Indian shops. Red lentils cook more quickly than green lentils.

TURMERIC

The dried, very yellow powder from a rhizome. Turmeric can stain so be careful when using it.

Vegetable Oil

I like to use peanut or corn oil for most of my cooking but you may use another oil if you prefer.

Yogurt

Indians use only plain yogurt in their cooking. This is unseasoned and unsweetened. Buy any plain yogurt that you like. The rich creamy ones as well as those made from skimmed milk will be quite satisfactory for my recipes.

INDEX

■■■■■■■

TABLE OF EQUIVALENTS
■■■■■■■

The exact equivalents in the following tables have been rounded for convenience.

US/UK
oz=ounce	tbl=tablespoon
lb=pound	fl oz=fluid ounce
in=inch	qt=quart
ft=foot	

Weights

US/UK	Metric
1 oz	30 g
2 oz	60 g
3 oz	90 g
4 oz (¼ lb)	125 g
5 oz (⅓ lb)	155 g
6 oz	185 g
7 oz	220 g
8 oz (½ lb)	250 g
10 oz	315 g
12 oz (¾ lb)	375 g
14 oz	440 g
16 oz (1 lb)	500 g
1½ lb	750 g
2 lb	1 kg
3 lb	1.5 kg

Liquids

US	Metric	UK
2 tbl	30 ml	1 fl oz
¼ cup	60 ml	2 fl oz
⅓ cup	80 ml	3 fl oz
½ cup	125 ml	4 fl oz
⅔ cup	160 ml	5 fl oz
¾ cup	180 ml	6 fl oz
1 cup	250 ml	8 fl oz
1½ cups	375 ml	12 fl oz
2 cups	500 ml	16 fl oz
4 cups/1 qt	1 l	32 fl oz

Metric
g=gram	cm=centimeter
kg=kilogram	ml=milliliter
mm=millimeter	l=liter

Length Measures

⅛ in	3 mm
¼ in	6 mm
½ in	12 mm
1 in	2.5 cm
2 in	5 cm
3 in	7.5 cm
4 in	10 cm
5 in	13 cm
6 in	15 cm
7 in	18 cm
8 in	20 cm
9 in	23 cm
10 in	25 cm
11 in	28 cm
12 in/1 ft	30 cm

Oven Temperatures

Fahrenheit	Celsius	Gas
250	120	½
275	140	1
300	150	2
325	160	3
350	180	4
375	190	5
400	200	6
425	220	7
450	230	8
475	240	9
500	260	10